TWAYNE'S WORLD AUTHORS SERIES

A Survey of the World's Literature

Sylvia E. Bowman, Indiana University

GENERAL EDITOR

FRANCE

Maxwell A. Smith, Guerry Professor of French, Emeritus
The University of Chattanooga
Former Visiting Professor in Modern Languages
The Florida State University

EDITOR

Ionesco

TWAS 239

TWAYNE'S WORLD AUTHORS SERIES (TWAS)

*The purpose of TWAS is to survey the major writers
—novelists, dramatists, historians, poets, philosophers,
and critics—of the nations of the world. Among the
national literatures covered are those of Australia,
Canada, China, Eastern Europe, France, Germany,
Greece, India, Italy, Japan, Latin America, the
Netherlands, New Zealand, Poland, Russia, Scan-
dinavia, Spain, and the African nations, as well as
Hebrew, Yiddish, and Latin Classical literatures. This
survey is complemented by Twayne's United States
Authors Series and English Authors Series.*

*The intent of each volume in these series is to present
a critical-analytical study of the works of the writer;
to include biographical and historical material that
may be necessary for understanding, appreciation,
and critical appraisal of the writer; and to present all
material in clear, concise English—but not to vitiate
the scholarly content of the work by doing so.*

CHAMPLAIN COLLEGE

Ionesco

By ALLAN LEWIS

University of Bridgeport

TWAYNE PUBLISHERS

A DIVISION OF G. K. HALL & CO., BOSTON

To Anita

Contents

Preface

When *The Bald Soprano, Chairs,* or *The Killer,* plays in which the theme of Nothingness courses through every line, finds increasing acceptance in the theatres of western civilization, it is apparent that Ionesco has touched something deep in contemporary malaise against which tradition cannot provide a protective sanctuary. For the Philistine to ignore the impact of Ionesco's work is to close his eyes to a significant moment in history when dependence on logic and scientific observation is no longer sufficient to provide satisfactory answers to persistent questions of purpose and direction. Reliance on Reason has generated unprecedented control over the physical forces of nature but has added little to the knowledge of man who is to exercise that control. The result has been a technological accumulation of awesome power and the continuing presence of poverty, war, alienation, and despair. Ionesco's surrealist mockery of the irrational consequences of the reign of Reason, ridiculing forces that were traditionally beyond human interference, provides the laughter that may be the forerunner to initiating new perspectives.

In his total war on Reason, Ionesco wisely rejects the weapons that Reason has provided for they eventually force the artist to accept self-defeating conditions for his own enslavement. He eliminates a logical time-space sequence of cause and effect relationships and devises his own techniques to portray the neglected world of the imagination. The result is an original drama which has had a profound influence on twentieth century theatre. The acceptance of Ionesco by an ever-increasing audience has provided its own ironic contradiction. In twenty years of literary activity, Ionesco has risen from a neglected avant-garde writer to international acclaim and membership in the French Academy.

The revolutionary has been encompassed by his own revolution. The logically based Establishment has taken its most pessimistic critic to its bosom and honored him as a responsible spokesman of the opposition.

The aim of this book is to trace the development of Ionesco's style and to analyze its component elements and inherent self-contradictions. The original intention was to discuss the major themes of Ionesco's work and to show how they reappear in all the plays. For the benefit of students and theatre workers who are concerned with individual plays, this plan was abandoned and the works are now presented in chronological order. Chapter Two remains a condensed version of the earlier plan.

Most of Ionesco's work, including the essays, are currently available in the authorized English translations of Donald Watson and Derek Prouse. Wherever some liberty has been taken with these translations, no footnote reference is given. For Ionesco's own critical comments on his work we have relied heavily on his *Notes and Counter Notes* and *Journal en miettes*. The plays of Ionesco, however, should be seen in the theatre for they have an additional stage dimension which the written text cannot supply.

ALLAN LEWIS

University of Bridgeport

Chronology

1957   *Le Nouveau Locataire* (*The New Tenant*), Théâtre d'Aujourd'hui, Paris, dir. Robert Postec.

1959   *Rhinocéros* (*Rhinoceros*), produced ‚in Düsseldorf, Germany, dir. K. H. Stroux.

      Tueur sans gages (*The Killer*), Théâtre Récamier, Paris, dir. Jose Quaglio.

1960   *Rhinocéros* (*Rhinoceros*), produced at the Théâtre de France, Paris, dir. Jean-Louis Barrault; London production directed by Orson Welles at the Royal Court Theatre with Laurence Olivier.

      Apprendre à marcher, ballet, Théâtre de l'Etoile, Paris.

      Tueur sans gages (*The Killer*), produced in New York.

1961   Wrote *La Colère*, sketch for the film *Les sept péchés capitaux*.

1962   *Délire à deux* (*Frenzy for Two*), Studio des Champs-Elysées, Paris, dir. Antoine Bourseiller.

      L'Avenir est dans les oeufs (*The Future Is in Eggs*), Théâtre de la Gaîté-Montparnasse, Paris, dir. Robert Postec.

      Le Roi se meurt (*Exit the King*), Théâtre de l'Alliance Française, Paris, dir. Jacques Mauclair.

      Wrote *Notes et Contre-Notes* (*Notes and Counter Notes*).

1963   *Le Piéton de l'air* (*Pedestrian of the Air*), produced in Düsseldorf, Germany. Paris production at Théâtre de France, dir. Jean-Louis Barrault.

1965   *La Soif et la faim* (*Hunger and Thirst*), produced in Düsseldorf, Germany.

1966   *La Soif et la faim* (*Hunger and Thirst*), Paris production at the Comédie-Française, dir. Jean-Marie Serreau.

1967   Published *Journal en miettes*.

1968   Published *Présent passé Passé présent*.

1970   *Jeux de massacre* (*Massacre Games*), produced in Düsseldorf, Germany. Paris production September 1970, Théâtre Montparnasse-Baston-Baty, dir. Jorge Lavelli. U.C. production Arena Stage, Washington, D.C., April, 1971.

1971   Elected to the Académie Française.

1972   *Macbett*, Théâtre Rive-Gauche, Paris, dir. Jacques Mauclair.

CHAPTER 1

The Limits of Reason

"Truth lies in our dreams."
(*Notes and Counter Notes*)

I *The Absurd*

THE plays of Eugène Ionesco represent the most thorough rejection of established order and the Rule of Reason. Causality, the logical relationship of one event to another, is logically absurd, for it eliminates the uncertainty of the human factor and the mystery of the universe, "the unfathomable third dimension which makes a whole man." [1] When causality is unpredictable any event may be the result of any other event regardless of time and space, and all events are equally insignificant. Science has created "automatic men speaking and behaving automatically," [2] living in the "emptiness of a world without metaphysics and a humanity without problems." [3] Truth is unknowable, for all is contradictory and the opposite of the seemingly true is equally valid. Direction and purpose vanish when science and reason are illusory and the individual is trapped in the contemplation of his own image. Man is reduced to a mess of contradictions, a good example of which is Ionesco's own life and work.

A Rumanian by birth, he lives in Paris and writes in French. In 1950 *The Bald Soprano* was presented at the Théâtre des Noctambules on the Left Bank with only three people in attendance. Fortunately for Ionesco, these three people were Armand Salacrou, Raymond Queneau and Roger Vitrac! Twenty years later *Hunger and Thirst* opened in Düsseldorf with the full diplomatic corps in attendance and wide critical acclaim for another Ionesco play demonstrating the futility of human effort. A neglected avantgarde writer had become the hero of the Establishment.

The crowning contradiction was the election of Ionesco in 1971 to the French Academy, alienating the young rebels who had hailed him as a prophet of negation; and he succeeded Jean Paulhan, a staid literary critic. Ionesco, preoccupied with death, had become an academician, one of the Forty Immortals. He espoused freedom of the imagination and opposed political commitment, yet in *Rhinoceros* he wrote one of the most devastating attacks against totalitarian conformity. He shatters traditional form, yet he sets up a pattern which is rigidly enforced. The theatre of the past he condemned as false and dishonest, concerned with the private neuroses of individual man, yet he dreams of a nostalgic Paradise, a forgotten Eden before the Age of Reason. Communication is no longer possible, yet Ionesco's plays are a method of communicating noncommunication.

To respond to Ionesco's world, where man is alone, deserted by God, relying on science and reason, which have proved to be illusory, caught in the adoration of things, which now reap their revenge, a world that as it rushes towards senseless annihilation can be represented only by a theatre equally mad, where the only certainty is death, the final act of absurdity, where symbols have to be found to express the total madness, it is helpful to place the current revolt against reason in historical perspective.

II *Descartes' Dualism*—"The non-metaphysical world
of today has destroyed all mystery."

If a villain in the piece is to be named, it might just as well be Descartes, who started it all in the seventeenth century with his famous dualism, which posited the scientific basic for a coherent universe. Feudalism, a civilization which had endured for a thousand years, gave way, under the impact of the Renaissance, to a world of change, motion, trade, manufacturing, and belief in the power of scientific observation to reveal the laws of nature. Descartes declared that the objective and measurable is real, that pain, suffering, anguish, love, are subjective and foreign to the realm of the rational. Man's progress on earth had formerly been measured by increased awareness of the Grand Design of God. Cause and effect now disclosed the manifestations of logical relationships which explained all phenomena. History was an onward progression of purpose. The theory worked and answered satisfactorily the doubts which had arisen from the breakdown of the formally structured medieval world of faith, obedience, and honor.

By the twentieth century, dependence on logic and causality had set in motion a complicated machinery that mastered the physical forces of nature and initiated a technological age of air conditioners, instant communication, computerized production, and long-range missiles with atomic warheads. The Great Chain of Being was replaced by Reason, which assumed the role of God and guided the destinies of man with purposeful determination; but the agonizing truth remained, that Reason had produced an irrational world of wars, poverty, racial hatred, and aggrandizement of nations. Presumed to liberate, science and technology had imposed dehumanizing restrictions. Man knew little more about himself, his purpose on earth, and the mystery of life. "The non-metaphysical world of today has destroyed all mystery, . . . alienating the unfathomable third dimension which makes a whole man." [4] Or in William Barrett's words:

> Science stripped nature of its human forms and presented man with a universe that was neutral, alien, in its vastness and force, to his human purpose. Religion, before this phase set in, had been a structure that encompassed man's life, providing him with a system of images and symbols by which he could express his own aspirations toward psychic wholeness. With the loss of this containing framework, man became not only a dispossessed but a fragmentary being. [5]

As a result, in the midst of material wealth and production capability man feels himself estranged from God, from nature, and from his own self, lost because of the incompetence of Reason to explore the deepest meanings of existence. Reason had presumed to be all of life, ignoring man as a self-transcendent animal who cannot be understood in his totality by the natural sciences and objective truth alone. Unanswered questions left a sense of the absurdity and contingency of human life and contributed to the collapse of the well-built logical structure, when as Yeats said in "The Second Coming," "Things fall apart; the centre cannot hold; Mere anarchy is loosed upon the world."

III   *The Revolt of the Irrational*—"One can never
penetrate another's identity."

Down with Reason was the new battle cry. Return to what had been ignored—the emotions, feelings, appetites, over which Reason had no control. Descartes' reliance on what could be measured and subjected to causal relationships had eliminated most of man, the vital intensity of the unmeasurable, man's instincts, experiences, and passions.

To dismiss the most central fact of man's being because it is inner and subjective is to make the hugest subjective falsification possible—one that leaves out the really critical half of man's nature. For without that underlying subjective flux, as experienced in floating imagery, dreams, bodily impulses, formative ideas, projections, and symbols, the world that is open to human experience can be neither described nor rationally understood.[6]

In contemporary art, the first to be discarded were the traditional assumptions of rational forms. To quote William Barrett again: "The modern artist sees man not as the rational animal in the sense handed down to the West by the Greeks, but . . . at the limits of Reason, one comes face to face with the meaningless; and the artist today shows us the absurdity, the inexplicable, the meaningless in our daily life."[7] In the theatre, all avant-garde movements have one common denominator, rejection of the realistic drama of plot, action, crises, and individual characters psychologically developed. Realism is regarded as the art form of a scientific age, for it presumes a time-space sequence of what is logical and coherent and characters that are definitely knowable.

The search was on for the discontinuous, the noncoherent, the discrete aspects of man's existence, which constitute his private world of being. At the end of the nineteenth century August Strindberg, who had mastered realism as a dramatic form, found it too limited to express the deeper anxieties of man. He presented onstage in his dream plays the illogic of the subconscious, the hidden truth in the disconnectedness of fancy, seeking to give dramatic shape to what had been formless. He was the first to explore a new set of symbols, the new language to express the inconceivable, the impossible, the imaginary, and the irrational. Luigi Pirandello followed at the time of the cataclysmic absurdity of the First World War with an attack on the very nature of reality itself, declaring truth to be endlessly relative and character endlessly unknowable. Actions of human beings are unpredictable, for one can never penetrate another's identity when beneath the assumed self lies another self equally indistinct. Pirandello had action take place on many levels simultaneously, with actors moving onstage, in the auditorium, and in the lobby, as well as up and down the aisles, a re-enactment of the process of living, surrounded by all the artifice of imposed and obvious theatricality, which could assume a truth of its own.

Alfred Jarry in his *Ubu Roi* plays presented grotesque surrealistic figures who like Jarry himself showed their contempt for the cruelty and stupidity of the universe by making their own lives a poem of incoherence and absurdity. Jarry died young, in filth and poverty, a victim of drugs. Years later he was enshrined as the Chancellor of the College of 'Pataphysicians, of which Ionesco is the Dean of Admissions. This mock institution devotes itself to the study of "the science of the particular, of the laws governing exceptions," [8] which means that every event is a law unto itself or that there is no law.

The revolt of the irrational is well-expressed in Antonin Artaud's *Theatre and Its Double* in which he coined the phrase, "the Theatre of Cruelty." To Artaud the realistic theatre was "a closed egoistic personal art." [9] He was interested not so much in the cruelty that results from violence and sadism as in the cruelty to one's nerve ends, the cruelty which induces trance, which affects the organism by physical means beyond control. He wanted a theatre of poetic images, audience shock, and communion of the spirit. He declared, "All our ideas about life must be revised in the period when nothing any longer adheres to life. It is this painful cleavage which is responsible for the revenge of things." [10]

All the arts responded in their opposition to limiting controls which Reason had exercised. The traditional modes were no longer adequate to express the perplexity and absurdity of the human condition. The dissolution of realism in postimpressionist

painting had given way to geometric design, surrealist grotes-
querie, and abstract patterns ranging from the Russian artist
Malevich's minimal art of white on white in 1905 to Mondrian's
severe line arrangements and Kandinsky's bursts of pure color.
Dada and surrealism had established the supremacy of the subconscious impulses in refashioning a superreality foreign to rational order. The uncertainty of truth led to emphasis on private
fantasy, a retreat to primitive drives, and the hallucinatory world
of psychedelic experiences.

In literature, James Joyce had explored the invention of new language forms to offset the restrictions of the logical and grammatical sequence of words. Kafka had depicted the strange terror of
the lost self in a bureaucratic and dehumanized social disintegration. In music, traditional tonality had given way to the eerie
clamor of electronic music and the dissonant rhythms of John
Cage. In dance, Merce Cunningham released the classical ballet
from its formal rigidity, freeing the body for a wider range of
emotional expression. The abandonment of psychological realism,
traditional logic, and inherited patterns of communication aimed
at restoring the lost sense of cosmic wonder to counteract an envi-
ronment that had become mechnical, sterile, and without dignity.

The drama was slower to respond, for it is a collective art re-
quiring the combined efforts of many arts and functions only
when an audience is able to respond instantaneously; but by the
late 1940s the stage was set. A host of new writers thrust the
theatre into the forefront of the revolt of the irrational. Among
them were Samuel Beckett, Jean Genet, Arthur Adamov, Michèl
de Ghelderode, Jacques Audiberti, Jean Tardieu, Georges
Schéhadé, Jean Vauthier, and Eugène Ionesco.

CHAPTER 2

The Development of a Style

"The non-historical . . . remains alive."

(Notes and Counter Notes)

OF all playwrights who reject the constrictions of reason, Samuel Beckett and Eugène Ionesco are the most influential. Both have moved from the passionate acclaim of a clamorous but small group of devotees to world attention. When Beckett won the Nobel Prize for Literature, Ionesco remarked, "We really deserved it." [1]

To Ionesco, the theatre of realism presupposes a logical, coherent universe which experience denies. The conflict between the assurance of order and the chaos of existence generates frustration, anxiety, and despair. Man's need for rational explanations is met by the passive indifference of the universe. The first step to freedom is to eliminate the hold that scientific logic has exerted on the mind and perception of man, to live without reliance on a benign God or godlike Reason. If what is experienced is determined by an inherited way of seeing, then the method of perception has to be altered. Emotions and felt experiences, love and hate and anguish, cannot be communicated when communication is regulated by rational rules. An algebraic formula cannot define the totality of man.

I *Beyond Realism*—"Realism . . . never looks beyond reality."

Realism, the dominant dramatic form of the first half of the twentieth century, is slavishly limited to what scientific order dictates. "Life as it is" can never be seen onstage unless the living is

19

done in the theatre, and even then it would be artificial, for it is one step removed from actual experience. Reality cannot be portrayed if the real is unknowable and subject to differing interpretations. Behind psychologically developed characters from Mrs. Alving in *Ghosts* to Willy Loman in *Death of a Salesman* lies a concept of human nature based on a belief in an ordered and knowable universe in which history has a meaning and a purposeful progression. Rejecting its techniques, however, involves a thorough revolution which invites chaos, for no standards remain by which judgment can be made. Imagination, transcendence, dreams, are not susceptible to translations in realistic terms. The theatre has to chose its own metaphysical reality, "to take into account our basic truths and our fundamental obsessions: love, death, astonishment. It [realism] presents man in a reduced and strange perspective. Truth is in our dreams, in the imagination." [2]

Man can be released from the absurdity which logical relationships have imposed upon him by discovering the fullness of human nature in the logic of dreams and the flow of the subconscious. Daisy in *Rhinoceros,* before she joins the herd and becomes a rhinoceros says, "There are many realities. Choose the one that's best for you. Escape into the world of the imagination." Ionesco once stated that he preferred that his plays be performed by young people because the young "in their unreason, reason rightly as opposed to the unreasonable reasoning of their elders." [3] In *The Killer* Bérenger, in the final confrontation with the enemy, finds traditional logic of no avail. Since he has no other means by which to comprehend the mysterious, he loses power over himself, drops his pistol, and becomes a helpless victim before the Killer's knife. He is unable to reach the unspoken mind of his foe, unprepared to reach understanding beyond reason.

The theatre to Ionesco is a means whereby the impossible can be explored and a trail blazed to reach another reality that has objective existence. This is the basic irony of Ionesco's work. The reality of a scientific world is unreal. "The search is for some essential reality, nameless and forgotten, and outside of which I do not feel I exist." [4] The characters in his plays are therefore grotesque and "derisively tragic," for they "drift through incoherence, having nothing of their own apart from their anguish, their remorse, their failures, the vacuity of their lives." [5] The characters in *The Bald Soprano* are interchangeable since mechanical repetition and computerized existence deny individuality.

Freedom from existing forms and in particular the realistic theatre, includes freedom from social commitment. If man's existence is irrational, no logical solution, political or social, can effect significant change.

> The non-metaphysical world of today has destroyed all mystery; and the so-called "scientific" theatre of the period, the theatre of politics and propaganda, anti-poetic and academic, has flattened mankind out, alienating the unfathomable third dimension which makes a whole man. The theatre of ideologies and theses, proposing political solutions and presuming to save humanity, actually saves no one. I have no wish to save humanity—to wish to save it, is to kill it—and there are no solutions. To realize that, is the only healthy solution. [6]

To Ionesco the "authentic human community is extra-social," held together by anxieties, desires, and secret nostalgias. Political solutions, whether of the Left or Right, flow from an effort to impose a substitute logical order and will as a necessary consequence impose a new tyranny. Revolutions flowing from good intentions turn into their opposites and become a "dogmatic stupidity of organized collective murder." Liberation becomes alienation, "the government, hateful power, abuse; justice, unleashed sadism." [7] This shift to opposites, the metamorphosis into the dialectical contradiction, is the record of history. "The wish becomes the anti-wish . . . the French Revolution declared its intention of establishing among other things equality. It firmly established inequality. Christianity wanted to establish peace and charity. It stirred up wrath and fury and perpetual war. It gave fresh cause for hatred." [8]

II   *The London Controversy*—"I have been judged . . . by dogmatic and ideological theologians."

Ionesco is thus strongly opposed to partisan political attachment. He refused to heed Sartre's call for all writers to declare themselves, to be committed to a party or a cause, to take their stand on social issues. For this he was taken to task by the distinguished English critic Kenneth Tynan, in what has now become a celebrated exchange of letters.

Kenneth Tynan had been one of Ionesco's staunchest supporters, but in June, 1958 he accused Ionesco of being totally removed from political decisions which could affect the future history of man, of continuing to participate in the destruction of all existing institutions, of adding to the feeling of helplessness and chaos and rejecting positive action by which a less absurd world could be created. He declared that while Ionesco offered an "escape from realism, it was an escape into a blind alley—a self-imposed vacuum wherein the author ominously bids us observe the absence of air. . . . Ionesco's theatre is pungent and exciting but it remains a diversion. It is not on the main road." [9] Ionesco could not resist a public rejoinder. Politics, he claimed, is what divides men and breeds misunderstanding. Commitment should be made to existence, to that which is "extra-social, the sadness, nostalgia, pain, anxieties, which no political system has been able to abolish." [10]

Orson Welles and Philip Toynbee, among others, joined in the attack, claiming that Ionesco's portrayal of the absurdly tragi-comic was dangerous, for it weakened resistance to reactionary political forces. The controversy delighted Ionesco, for it offered the opportunity to attack advocates of particular ideologies which he considered illusory and deceptive, providing no solution other than the substitution of an equally absurd tyranny; but his responses underscored the contradictions of his own position. To answer advocates of political change he had to resort to language and logic which he always contended were unable to communicate beyond language and logic. He is more effective as an artist than as a polemicist. As for critics in general, he added, "Once upon a time I was a critic myself. I wrote a series of articles about a great poet from a foreign country. Step by step I took his work to pieces, in order to show that it had no value. These articles gave rise to much polemical discussion. Then, some weeks later, I wrote a fresh series of articles in order to prove that this poet had written nothing but masterpieces." [11]

To his opponents' claim that continued portrayal of despair and disorder eliminated hope, Ionesco replied with a searing attack on Bertolt Brecht and Marxist revolutionary doctrine. "The more I see of Brecht's plays the more I have the impression that time, *and* his own time, escape him; Brechtian man is shorn of one dimension, the writer's sense of period is actually falsified by his ideology, which narrows his field of vision; this is a fault common to ideologists and people stunted by fanaticism." [12]

To Ionesco, imaginative truth reaches beyond everyday reality, avoiding reducing man to algebraic formula and the historical variations of the moment. Man is not simply a social animal, "a prisoner of his time," but an enduring essence. The assumed normal world, the forms which hold society together, the state, the civil service, the police, the army, the educational apparatus, are elements in a logical order established by the bourgeois mind to diminish man, and they have proved disastrous. Alternatives, including the metaphysical, may be equally false and problematic, but they are worth exploring. Ionesco contended that his critics had fallen victim to political prejudices, and he commented wryly, "I feel I have been judged not by literary critics but by dogmatic and ideological theologians of every creed." [13] He was not interested in saving mankind or proving that "some men are better than others," [14] but in annihilating a logical system which distorts reality, and which has reduced man to his present tragi-comic posture.

III *Politics and Art*—"It is the dreamer . . . who is the revolutionary, who tries to change the world."

The artist should speak through his art, not through public debate, and though he had participated in the controversy, Ionesco's parting shot was a wry regret that he had tried to give an answer, that he had "constructed theories and talked too much when it was my business simply to 'invent' and pay no attention to the touts who kept tugging at my sleeve." [15]

The function of the avant-garde movement is to alter the consciousness of man, to overthrow outworn mental habits. In art this revolution is expressed in the movement from cubism to abstractionism. Revolution in art is "untopical" and sets itself against traditional ways of perception. A good example is Father Robert's description of Roberta I. "She's got green pimples on her beige skin, red breasts on a mauve background, an illuminated navel, a tongue the color of tomato sauce, pan-browned square shoulders and all the meat needed to merit the highest commendation." [16] This hardly answers to the Victorian concept of beauty, but it is close to Picasso and De Kooning.

The constant paradox pursues Ionesco. He reaches beyond the void in which all sense data are arbitrary and despite his protestations to the contrary does take a definite political position. *The Bald Soprano* is a powerful indictment of the sterility of bourgeois life and has given rise to innumerable imitations, including Edward Albee's *The American Dream*. Jean in *Hunger and Thirst* is a mythic antihero, the epitome of bourgeois discontent, who leaves hearth and home in search of ill-defined goals, all motion and no substance. *Rhinoceros* is an indictment of herd psychology and blind conformity, which establishes the basis for dictatorship. Mother Peep in *The Killer* is a terrifying example of Gestapo regimentation. The Professor in *The Lesson* puts on a Nazi armband after he has killed his fortieth pupil. Not specific issues, but the entire inheritance of Descartes' dualism is the focus of Ionesco's attack. "Shakespeare is always far more contemporary than Victor Hugo; Pirandello far more 'avant-garde' than Roger Ferdinand; Büchner infinitely more poignant and alive than, for example, Bertolt Brecht and his imitators in Paris." [17]

In an intellectual exercise, Ionesco took on all his critics in the overwritten but pointed *Improvisation or the Shepherd's Chameleon* (*L'Impromptu de l'Alma*), in which Bartholomeus I, II, and III represent the three schools of formal criticism, Kenneth Tynan, Bertolt Brecht, and the French classicists, who condemn Ionesco from preconceived standards, insensitive to anything that does not conform to their learned or not-so-learned views: "Those engaged or enraged critics who positively refuse to accept you as you are; some because of their own theories, some because of their fixed mental habits, and others because of their temperament or their allergies, in other words for subjective reasons, that are less complex and more fanciful." [18] Ordinary understanding remains on a level of consciousness distinct from that required for a work of art.

Critics impose preset value judgments denying the work of art its own existence on "a separate level of expression." [19] When asked to explain *Victims of Duty* Ionesco replied that to explain it "I would have had to write another play. That is to say, I would have written another series of images. . . ." [20]

IV   *A New Form and Content*—"I'm all for contradiction."

When asked why he wrote plays, Ionesco replied, "I feel very awkward and have no idea what to answer. Sometimes it seems to me I started writing for the theatre because I hated it." [21] Such remarks are not to be taken too seriously, for Ionesco wrote later, "When I had written something for the theatre, quite by chance and with the intention of holding it up to ridicule, I began to love it, to rediscover it in myself, to understand it, to be fascinated by it." [22] But to contradict even that statement he confessed later that when he said he really loved the theatre he had done so only to please the critics and the actors. [23]

Ionesco's technique for discovering his own world of native intuition, "creating a world which the creator discovers for himself," [24] is consistently developed in all his work from *The Bald Soprano* in 1950 to *Massacre Games* in 1970, evolving a style that is recognizable and distinctly personal. The early plays, *The Lessons, Jack or the Submission, The Chairs, Amédée,* are more static single conceits. The later full-length plays, *Rhinoceros, The Killer, Pedestrian of the Air, Hunger and Thirst,* contain more plot and are expositions of a theme, but the devices do not vary. Logical time and space do not exist. The Cartesian universe is absent. Accepted logic no longer prevails. In *The Bald Soprano* time is capricious and uncertain.

FIRE CHIEF:	It depends on what time it is.
MRS. SMITH:	We don't have the time, here.
FIRE CHIEF:	But the clock?
MR. SMITH:	It runs badly. It is contradictory, and always indicates the opposite of what the hour really is. [25]

If time is indefinite, so is age. Bérenger in *The Killer* says, "I could be sixty years old, seventy, eighty, a hundred and twenty, how do I know? . . . Time is above all subjective." Age depends on his emotional state or his relationship to his surroundings. In a timeless world of relative values all distinctions are equally senseless. The wife of Bobby Watson is also called Bobby Watson. "Since they both had the same name, you never could tell one from the other when you saw them together. It was only after his death that you could really tell which was which. And there are still people today who confuse her with the deceased and offer their condolences to him." [26]

Death does not remove the dead. The corpse in *Amédée* keeps growing. Space is not defined by physical limits. Jean in *Hunger and Thirst* walks through the Wall of Knowledge into the Good Inn of the Black Masses. Bérenger in *Pedestrian of the Air* leaves the ground and flies off to worlds beyond. The invisible furniture in *The Chairs* occupies the entire stage. The multiplication is at one and the same time "the absence of chairs, a proliferation and an emptiness." [27]

Abolish the hierarchy of rational order and all events are self-contradictory. Ionesco employs the device of contradictions, comic and grotesque, in endless variation, the trivial and the sublime equally weighted. "I'm all for contradiction," says Ionesco in *Improvisation*. "Everything is nothing but contradiction." [28] When Peter Hall, the director of the Royal Shakespeare Company, wanted to present *The Lesson*, which he had only read in English, he complained to Ionesco that the translation must be bad for the play was idiotic, to which Ionesco replied, "It is the text that is idiotic, that's the way I wrote it." [29] Contradictions need not offer synthesis, but if they are ever-present unrelieved pessimism should be balanced by a lighter note. Ionesco is consistently inconsistent. His plays offer little hope, yet he did say that "although existence is intolerable, painful, wearisome and stultifying" there is always present "the glorious manifestation of divine light." [30] It is an unusual confession of religious faith.

V   *The Tragedy of Language*—"Philology leads to calamity."

The breakdown of existing logic implies the death knell of language and grammatical construction, the instrument of logical communication. Words are reduced to empty sounds and the platitude becomes a revelation of fresh insight. Inherited language patterns can only convey the sense of absurd relationships. Ionesco stresses banality, repetitions, incongruity, and exaggerations in the manner of surrealist paintings. When he wrote *The Bald Soprano* he did not know how the play would end, but he did have in mind "the final breakdown of language and the resulting deterioration." [31]

The two couples in *The Bald Soprano* explode in a rhythmic chant of nonsense syllables using the letters of the alphabet as a choral refrain. Language is worn and tired: "separated from life . . . it is not so much necessary to reinvent it as to restore it." [32] Entire scenes are constructed from alternating disconnected clichés, as in *The Bald Soprano:*

> MR. SMITH: One walks on his feet, but one heats with electricity or coal.
> MR. MARTIN: He who sells an ox today, will have an egg tomorrow.
> MRS. SMITH: In real life, one must look out of the window.
> MRS. MARTIN: One can sit down on a chair, when the chair doesn't have any.[33]

Nuances of expression give way to a succession of platitudes. To the Professor in *The Lesson* all languages are identical. The word "cat" is all Roberta in *Jack* needs to express all concepts. The Old Man in *The Chairs* greets the Emperor with a humble obeisance and a dog's bark, "Your servant, your slave, your dog, arf, arf, your dog, Your Majesty." [34]

Language is a weapon of a logical world to precipitate destruction. The Maid in *The Lesson* advises the Professor that "philology leads to calamity." Bérenger, facing the Killer, exhausts all the devices of language to reason with his enemy, who responds not with words but with variations of chuckles until Bérenger is left speechless and helpless, a victim of the failure of words. The human voices in *Rhinoceros* are stilled and only animal grunts are heard. Jean in *Hunger and Thirst* is reduced to listing the names of things in a ritual of recalled experiences. The Old Man in *The Chairs* shouts to the waiting but invisible world that he has discovered "absolute certainty," a parody of the scientific pronouncement of first causes and ultimate enlightenment. The speech is delivered by a deaf-mute who can only grunt.

If sound can induce tragedy, silence becomes an effective dramatic opposite and the interchange of the two is developed in planned orchestration. Ionesco, like Beckett, uses broken sentences, half phrases, monologues, and sudden pauses to intensify the surrounding climate of nothingness.

VI   Characters—"Personality doesn't exist."

Where time and space do not respond to the Grand Design, it follows that characters cannot know their own identity nor that of others. Nicolas D'Eu in *Victims of Duty* says, "We'll get rid of the principle of identity and unity of character and let movement and dynamic psychology take its place . . . We are not ourselves . . . Personality doesn't exist." [35] Names, which in realistic drama represent family honor and the specific individuality of a man, cease to have meaning. Young and old, male and female are Bobby Watson. Characters shift, multiply, coalesce, split and converge as they do in Strindberg's dream plays. The Old Woman in *The Chairs* is wife, mother, and mistress. Madeleine in *Victims of Duty* is all women metamorphosed into housewife, seductive paramour, and old lady. The Concierge in *The Killer* doubles as Mother Peep, the Architect is also the Chief of Police, Roberta I is Roberta II and III, with one, two, and three noses. Characters become mechanical devices, uttering similar lines, since variations in language do not denote variations in personality. Psychological and emotional differences are eliminated as universal fears and hidden terrors obsess all characters.

VII   The Revenge of Things—"to bring objects to life"

Since material accumulation is an obsession of contemporary life, props are as important as characters or language. Things proliferate, take their revenge, dominate people, perform with their own intensity. The furniture in *The New Tenant* piles higher and higher until there is no place for the tenant, briefcases accumulate in *The Killer,* invisible chairs occupy all space in *The Chairs.* Coffee cups abound in *Victims of Duty,* serving plates in *Hunger and Thirst,* baskets full of eggs in *The Future is in Eggs,* multiple corpses in *Massacre Games.*

Nothing is barred in the theatre: characters may be brought to life, but the unseen presence of our inner fears can also be materialized. So the author is not only allowed, but recommended to make actors of his props, to bring objects to life, to animate the scenery and give symbols concrete form.[36]

Strange human mutations occur, transformation of people into rhinoceroses or the appearance of green hair and noses in *Jack.* Ionesco was fully aware of the danger of having objects and devices overwhelm the script. "If there are too many devices and mechanical movements there is too little life and it becomes suffocating." [37] The "too little life" does not apply only to people, but to things as well. Freud and Marx are banished in a parade of puppets which reveals through objects the mechanization of life and the absence of motivation.

VIII   *The Vision of the Past*—"Men have lost the peace of mind they had in the past."

Life has not always been so mechanical and dreary. Ionesco repeatedly refers to a nostalgic past when presumably communication, identity, and vitality of the passions were possible: a Lost Paradise, a Radiant City which predates the control of reason, a vision of luminous primitive glory before scientific limitations framed a sterile mechanical man unable to let dreams flow freely. The references to a past age of light render present darkness more insufferable. Discussing a pleasant early boyhood adventure, Ionesco said, "For me that will always be the image of a lost paradise. I abandoned it to go to Paris and later to Rumania. It then grew further away both in time and in space." [38] It did return and appeared in many of the plays. Choubert in the opening lines of *Victims of Duty* says, "It's the times we live in; all nerves. Nowadays men have lost the peace of mind they had in the past." [39] He wants to turn back the clock to retreat from their withered love to "magic gardens and flowers of fire in the night," but "suddenly it

was winter and ours is now an empty road. . . . The enchanted
garden has folded into night, has sunken into the mud." [40]

The colored lights, the visions of an incandescent past, of a time
when love held back time, may never have existed. The Lost Paradise may be illusory, another trick of the imagination, as unreli-
able as the fragmentary and contradictory perceptions of the
senses. The magic garden of the Old Couple in *The Chairs* was
Paris, but the Old Woman replies, "Paris never existed, my little
one," and the Old Man counters with: "That city must have existed because it collapsed . . . It was the city of light, but it has
been extinguished, for four hundred thousand years." The three
Bérengers of the later plays represent more fully developed
aspects of the return to a glorious past, the vision of the Radiant
City in *The Killer,* the flight into other worlds to discover the
source of the fireworks in *Pedestrian of the Air,* and the long pilgrimage in *Hunger and Thirst* that ends in menial servitude to the
Monks of the Inn. Each Bérenger encounters the evil in the Garden of Eden, the counterpointed pain and doubt and uncertainty.
The Lost Paradise, both luminous and menacing, is joyous and
threatening, full of bright stars and entrapping slime, the garden
that begins the fall of man.

Marriage as an institution contributes to the degradation of love
and the destruction of the golden image. Choubert sorrowfully
dreams of the time when Madeleine's body was in bloom and
when love was young, before marital relations warped and
maimed human association. Love is irrational, and sweeps beyond
controls and communication. The impulses of sex open onto a
world of mystery and promise, but domestic boredom is discord-
ant and corrosive. Marie in *Hunger and Thirst,* one of the few
faithful and loving women in Ionesco's plays, is willing to see
beauty in the dark and dismal place in which they live, but Jean
rushes off to find light beyond. Madeleine II is more typical as she
responds to Amédée II in shrill cries of pain, "Don't come near
me . . . you hurt me." In the rational world sexual expression appears grotesque, as in *The Lesson* when the Professor rapes the
Pupil with a knife, or sadistic, as in *Victims of Duty* when Madeleine calmly observes the brutal treatment of her husband by the
intruding Detective.

IX   *Death*—"We are made to be immortal, yet we die."

The final theme that pervades Ionesco's work is the fear of death and its total senselessness. In *Journal en miettes* he wrote: "One dies of hunger, one dies of thirst, one dies of boredom, one dies of laughter, one dies of envy, one dies every day." [41] But the everyday dying is the harrowing world of reality. The final release is irrational for it may come at any time, unexpected and unsolicited, the one aspect of life for which Reason has found no satisfactory answer. An entire play, *Exit the King*, is devoted to awaiting death or rather the anxiety in facing death. In *Massacre Games* the unknown plague strikes at everyone as corpses pile onstage in a ritual reenactment of the death of civilization.

Ionesco is constantly disturbed by the mortality of man, which is the ultimate paradox of an illogical existence. If life is totally senseless, the release from it should be welcome, yet life persists and has to be defended. The Architect in *The Killer* says, "If we thought about all the misfortunes of mankind we could never go on living. And we must live!" Ionesco, like all poets, is in search of immortality, yet the best he can achieve is to join the French Academy, the haven of the Forty Immortals, a meaningless title, for most of the academicians have long since been forgotten. Death in the plays is not presented in the macabre terms of serious tragedy, but made more terrifying by treating it as comedy. Exaggeration, paradox, contradiction, breakdown of language, surrealist images, attend the presence of death in grotesque distortions.

Ionesco does not conceal his theatrical devices but makes them more apparent. Yet he fully recognizes the point at which they can become antidramatic. "If there are too many devices and mechanical movements, there is too little of life and it becomes suffocatingly tragic because one gets the impression that the world has escaped the spirit." [42] The manner in which Ionesco's concepts are worked out in dramatic form follows in the detailed consideration of the separate plays.

CHAPTER 3

The Bald Soprano, The Lesson, The Chairs

> "All the committed authors want to rape us."
>
> (*Fragments of a Journal*)

I   *The Bald Soprano*—"characters emptied of psychology"

IONESCO'S first play, *The Bald Soprano* (*La Cantatrice Chauve,* 1950), set the tone for an entirely new concept of drama, anti-plays designed not only to indicate the emptiness of middle-class domestic life, which had been a persistent theme of bohemian rebels of the nineteenth century, but also to underscore the uselessness of writing plays. The obvious self-contradiction, a play that is an anti-play, ushered in a decade of language inventiveness, surrealist metaphors, and non-Aristotelian devices, which as satire, travesty, and tongue-in-cheek hoax, upset all the long held notions of the nature of drama.

The Bald Soprano opened at the Théâtre des Noctambules on May 11, 1950 on a rainy Sunday night with the roof of the theatre leaking and an audience of three people. Twenty years later, the play was still being performed in a *théâtre de poche* on the Left Bank of Paris and has been seen in theatres all over the world and been incorporated into the required selections of most repertory companies. When a play, despite an inglorious opening night, can command the attention of an increasingly large audience in the Western World, a play in which the theme of nothingness runs through every scene, it is safe to conclude that it has touched a responsive chord in the conscience of an age and reflects the deep anxieties of a particular moment in history.

In my first play, *The Bald Soprano,* which started off as an attempt to parody the theatre, and hence a certain kind of human behavior, it

33

was by plunging into banality, by draining the sense from the hollowest clichés of everyday language that I tried to render the strangeness that seems to pervade our whole existence.[1]

The characters are without character, mechanical puppets. Time does not exist and plot is absent, as are suspense and heightened movement. The language is a rising crescendo of platitudes that erupts in the final ritual of embattled couples into a choral chant of nonsense syllables. No order prevails. Nothing is sacred. Communication is expressed in animal grunts. Marital bliss is reduced to a caterwauling of equally empty computerized partners. Yet the audience laughs, which surprised Ionesco, or at least he pretended to be surprised. An exposé of the pettiness and triviality of domestic relations, of the routine responses that deny emotional or imaginative vitality, "of words turned into sounding shells devoid of meaning, characters emptied of psychology," [2] was intended as a caustic comment on the common experience of all. The bitter joke is that the audience was laughing at its own vacuity.

The scene is a middle-class English interior, completely English. Mr. and Mrs. Smith are seated in the living room after dinner. As he is reading a newspaper she is knitting English socks. After a moment of English silence, "the English clock strikes seventeen English strokes." [3]

The dialogue is a series of non sequiturs and illogicalities, a reduction to absurdity of everyday conversation, as though one had taken a recording of what was said in a bus or suburban train and played it back as a mélange of inconsequential inanities. Mr. Smith reads in the paper that Bobby Watson has just died. Bobby Watson turns out to be the name also of the dead man's widow as well as the name of the children, the uncle, the cousin, and almost everyone else. To the realistic playwright an individual's name is the symbol of his identity. Arthur Miller in *The Crucible* and *A View From The Bridge* has his protagonist go to his death rather than disgrace his name. In Renaissance literature, a man's name implies a duty to uphold its honor. With the breakdown of tradition, Ionesco discards the significance of separate individuality. In the surrealist logic of fancy, names shift and characters merge.

As to Bobby Watson, the surviving wife, Mrs. Smith asks if she is pretty, and Mr. Smith replies, "She has regular features and yet one cannot say that she is pretty. She is too big and stout. Her features are not regular but still one can say that she is very pretty. She is a little too small and too thin." [4] Contradiction follows contradiction, for in the absence of objective criteria the opposite of a statement is equally true. "To liberate his obsessions an author has only one duty, to let his fantasies take shape without intervention from any source." [5]

Mr. and Mrs. Martin, the dinner guests, arrive and are attracted to each other. They discover that they live on the same street, in the same house, sleep in the same bed, and have the same child, a bizarre coincidence, since the girl is blonde and has a white eye and a red eye. Mr. Martin ends this interlude in a flat monotonous voice, saying, "Then, dear lady, I believe that there can be no doubt about it, we have seen each other before and you are my own wife . . . Elizabeth I have found you again." [6] Ionesco is not only mocking the standard melodrama of intrigue and romantic adventure and the usual love scenes, but he is also parodying the failure of love, the emptiness of marriage wherein husband and wife are unable to know each other. Love belongs to the world beyond reason and has never been understood by the Smiths and the Martins with their reasoned conformity, which cannot explore the mysterious unknown of the emotions. The two couples sit facing each other. The conversation, replete with silences and accelerated rhythms, is hollow and automatic. Any event, death, or reading from a newspaper is uttered with equal emphasis, and greeted with comparable enthusiasm.

The doorbell rings three times and each time Mrs. Smith goes to the door and finds no one there. The fourth time Mr. Smith answers the bell and the Fire Chief enters. Mrs. Smith, on the basis of experience, maintains that when the doorbell rings no one is there. Mr. Smith on the other hand, a defender of cause-and-effect logic, insists that when the doorbell rings someone is always there. The Fire Chief, who also acts as a confessor, settles the argument by stating that "when the doorbell rings, sometimes there is someone, and other times there is no one," an example of the way in which logic can clarify experience. They then play a game of storytelling, each recounting an experimental fable of weird geographical and physiological disconnections. Mary, the Maid, who turns out to be the lover of the Fire Chief, recites a poem in his honor which ends with "irrefutable truisms." [7]

> The smoke caught fire
> The fire caught fire
> Everything caught fire
> Caught fire, caught fire. [8]

As the Fire Chief is about to leave, Mrs. Martin thanks him for helping them pass "a truly Cartesian quarter of an hour," to which he replies, "Speaking of that—the bald soprano?" This is the only reference to the title in the play. Years later in *Pedestrian of the Air* Ionesco made up for this omission by introducing a bald soprano who walks across the stage and disappears. He had originally intended to call his first play *English Made Easy* or *The English Hour*, but when the director Nicolas Bataille said that the play might be taken as a satire on English middle-class life, the title was changed for the reason that "no prima donna with or without hair appears in the play," a delightful disregard for logical coherence. Ionesco added later that an actor playing the Fire Chief made a slip of the tongue and instead of saying "*institutrice blonde*" said "*cantatrice chauve*," and a title was discovered. This, however, seems too logical to be accurate.

The two couples, after the Maid and the Fire Chief have left, engage in a fast-moving interchange of assorted platitudes, aphorisms and non sequiturs, which gather momentum in rapid-fire nonsense syllables such as: "Mice have lice, lice haven't mice," "Don't ruche my broach!" "Don't smooch the brooch!" "Groom the goose, don't goose the broom." The rhythm increases, the letters of the alphabet, vowels and consonants alternating, explode in a final outburst and blackout. When the lights come up, the Smiths or, if the director chooses, the Martins, are in the same position as when the play opened, carrying on the same conversation, and the action starts all over again, indicating the continuing emptiness, the ongoing sameness, the purposeless passions of "people who have no hunger, no conscious desires. They are bored stiff, but people who are unconsciously alienated don't even know they are bored, they feel it vaguely, hence the final explosion which is quite useless as the characters and situations are both static and interchangeable and everything ends where it started." [9]

The play has no apparent content but "simply theatrical machinery functioning in a void." [10] The people of *The Bald Soprano* can be substituted for one another, since they are all the same person, or nonexistent persons, people with no problems, since they live in a world without "metaphysics, where all social problems have been resolved, . . . the world of tomorrow." [11]

How the play came to be written is an indication of Ionesco's seriocomic attitude. He wanted to learn English and bought an *"English-French Conversational Manual for Beginners."* He discovered that instead of learning English he was discovering "some very surprising truths, . . . that the floor is below us, the ceiling above us, that there are seven days in the week," which he had known before but which were now seen as "indisputably true." In the textbook, when the Martins in Lesson Five join their friends the Smiths they say, "The country is more peaceful than big cities," "Yes, but cities are more highly populated and there are more shops," a revelatory series of contrasting truths that gave Ionesco the basis of his dialogue. [12]

Even though the non-end to this anti-play represents a cyclical repetition of continuing senselessness, Ionesco had considered other possible endings, including one in which during the final quarrel the audience would invade the stage and the manager and superintendent of police would come on and fire at the audience with live ammunition "to make an example of them," after which the police, guns in hand, would order the theatre cleared.

The Bald Soprano has been interpreted as a criticism of bourgeois society, a parody of realistic drama, a satire on English life, a mock-surrealist farce, an assault on methods of learning foreign languages, a comment on the lack of communication. Ionesco accepted all such interpretations, even contradictory ones, but did admit that the play is "about a kind of universal petite bourgeoisie, the petit bourgeois being a man of fixed ideas and slogans, a ubiquitous conformist, which is revealed in his mechanical language." [13]

The Bald Soprano is a demonstration of life's utter banality, unconscious boredom, and serious nonsense, exposing with "the tragedy of language" the monstrous forms within us deposited by a lifeless morality.

II   *The Lesson*

The second short play also has the action start all over again after the curtain has fallen, which according to Ionesco is more realistic than the realistic dramas which end with a resolution of opposing forces or a choice of alternative solutions. Unlike that of *The Bald Soprano,* the title of *The Lesson* (*La Leçon,* 1951) refers to what happens onstage. *The Lesson* is actually about a lesson.

A lively, dynamic young girl of eighteen comes to the Professor for tutorial help in preparation for "the total doctorate." As the Professor, a little old man, age sixty, timid and proper, proceeds with the lesson, the pupil grows increasingly sad, tired, and withdrawn, unable to speak, completely passive. She becomes the paralyzed victim of the Professor, who changes from the mild, polite teacher to a lewd, dominating, aggressive tyrant. His voice grows imperceptively more assured and sonorous as hers grows increasingly inaudible. The lesson ends as the Professor plunges a knife, real or imaginary, into the pupil's body in a symbolic rape and murder. The Maid rebukes the Professor, reminding him that this is his fortieth victim and he soon may run out of pupils. He protests, "She didn't want to learn! She was disobedient!" [14] As the Professor shows signs of fear, the Maid places an armband, preferably with a Nazi insignia on his arm, saying, "Wear this, then you won't have anything more to be afraid of. That's good politics." [15] As the body is removed, the bell rings and the forty-first pupil enters to start the same procedure all over again.

The actual lesson begins with general knowledge, naming the capital of France and listing the four seasons, which the pupil has difficulty doing. They then turn to arithmetic. The pupil shows some skill in addition but cannot subtract three from four. The Professor admonishes her, "You always have a tendency to add. But one must be able to subtract too. It's not enough to integrate, you must also disintegrate. That's the way life is. That's philosophy.

That's science. That's progress, civilization." [16] The Professor is a master at disintegration and shifts to philology despite the Maid's warning that "philology leads to calamity." As the Professor explains the origins of words and sounds and linguistic correlatives in all languages, "for the word 'Italy,' in French we have the word 'France,' which is an exact translation of it," [17] the pupil complains of a toothache, raising a responsive chant to the Professor's continuing declamation. The interaction between the two culminates in the learning of all the translations of the word "knife." The Professor brandishes an invisible knife, circling around the suffering student in a tribal dance, pronouncing the word in ascending rhythms counterpointed by the pupil's cries as the pain enters her head, her throat, her neck, her thighs, her breast. As the knife penetrates her body, she falls over on the chair in an indecent posture, her legs spread wide as the Professor accomplishes his lust for power and total demoralization of a victim.

Contradictions multiply as the basis of Ionesco's technique. The Professor is logically clear in simple arithmetic but when he turns to comparative linguistics, his speciality, he, who is charged with achieving communication, is thoroughly unintelligible. His power is a combination of intellectual and physical hypnotism. Sex, a means of communication in life, leads to death. The pupil offers some resistance, which only arouses the Professor to greater lengths of criminality. As in *The Bald Soprano*, the ringing of bells is the musical invitation to an absence of causality, since noncharacters are involved in a demonstration of all communication as frustratingly absurd.

To actors, Ionesco supplied the advice that since they too are similar to the characters in the play, all they need do is act themselves; but since the play is a burlesque pushed beyond its extreme limits in "imperceptible transitions" he added more specific suggestions. "A burlesque text, play it dramatic. A dramatic text, play it burlesque. Make words say things they never meant." [18]

If communication is meaningless, education is illusory, handing on useless knowledge which further limits freedom. The serious side of this comic drama sees the Professor as a totalitarian oppressor and brutal criminal imparting information to shackle the mind and erase individuality, but he has the willing complicity of

the Pupil. Passion and pain strive to resist logic, but they are in-
struments for arousing further resentment on the part of the oppressor. García Lorca, in *Blood Wedding,* uses the knife as a folk
symbol of fertility and death, a giver of life and the means of
taking life. When outworn social conditions turn its edge to killing
and revenge, the knife becomes a symbol of the triumph of confusion, political, sexual, and linguistic.

III   *The Chairs*

Ionesco called *The Chairs* (*Les Chaises,* 1952) a "tragic-farce,"
another example of the juxtaposition of opposites. The setting is a
circular room atop a tower, surrounded by water, a setting for the
wasted, isolated, mediocre lives of the Old Man, aged ninety-five,
and the Old Woman, aged ninety-four, who are the only characters until the entrance of the Orator at the end. The opening lines
are about a "bad smell from . . . stagnant water," the world
around them. The Old Woman wants to watch the boats in the
sunlight and is told that it is nighttime. They review their past as
childhood scenes merge with the present and the future. The Old
Woman cradles her man in her lap, the return to the womb, and
they play games such as imitating the months, the visual form of
nonsense. The Old Man's words when he refers to Paris may even
suggest Ionesco's prediction that the world is threatened with
atomic annihilation. "It was the city of light"—he uses the past
tense—"but it has been extinguished, for four hundred thousand
years . . . Nothing remains of it today, except a song." The Old
Woman asks "What song?" and the Old Man replies, "A lullaby,
an allegory: 'Paris will always be Paris.' "

As they tell their past, the syncopated speech changes to a slow,
dreamy rhythm. Words vanish into multiple meanings in Joycean
fashion. The Old Man sits in his wife's lap and wets, moaning,
"I'm all spoiled, . . . my career is spilled." Platitudes of success
flow in and around their tale of failure. Many guests have been
invited to hear the final message of the Old Man, his vindication.
The couple speak to the visitors as they arrive, arrange seats for
them, interrupt conversations. The stage becomes full of chairs,
until finally the Emperor enters. All the guests are imaginary and
invisible, but idle chatter, flirtations, arguments with all of them,

and the Old Man's hopes make them real. The scene rises to the animation of a dynamic ballet with the placing of the chairs, the music of doorbells, the sounds of the boats—all leading up to the great message of freedom from the misunderstood intellectual. So full of people is the imagined stage that the Old Man and Woman get lost in the crowd, and when the Old Man finds her, he says, "I am not myself. I am another. I am the one in the other"— an echo of Rimbaud's concept of the division of self, but here used also to show the sameness of all.

The Old Man seeks certainty and truth in the midst of the absurd. Now that the Emperor is present, the Old Man can at last have the Orator deliver his message. His life "has been filled to overflowing." He will not have lived in vain. His words will be revealed to the world. Conscious that all has been arranged, or unable to undo the complications of their own plans, the Old Man and Woman leap out of the window to their deaths as the Orator moves to the lectern. He, the only other real person in the play, stands before the nonexistent assemblage and delivers to posterity the great message: "[*He faces the rows of empty chairs; he makes the invisible crowd understand that he is deaf and dumb; . . . then he coughs, groans, utters the guttural sounds of a mute*]: He, mme, mm, mm. Ju, gou, hou, hou. Heu, heu, gu, gou, gueue." [19] Unable to speak, he writes on the blackboard: "AN-GELFOOD," then mutters more unintelligible sounds, erases what he has written, and replaces it with the word "ADIEU." The futility of life and the inability to communicate have rarely been dramatized so graphically. Ionesco wrote: "In 'The Chairs' I have tried to deal with the themes that obsess me; with emptiness, with frustration, with this world, at once fleeting and crushing, with despair and death. The characters I have used are not fully conscious of their spiritual rootlessness, but they feel it instinctively and emotionally." [20]

To express the gap between aspiration and achievement, between dreams and arbitrary indifference to human concerns, the "vacuity of reality, language and human thought," Ionesco urged his first director to "let this vacuity slowly invade the stage, continually covering up with words used like clothes, the absence of real people." The use of contradictions is essential in the production as it is in the text. "What is needed is plenty of gesture, almost pantomime, lights on, moving objects, doors that open and close, and open again, in order to create this emptiness so that it grows and devours everything. Absence can only be created in opposition to things present." [21]

The Bald Soprano and *The Lesson* created minor scandals. For *The Chairs* in 1952, the third play to be presented in Paris, eight rather uncomfortable people attended the evening performance, but the controversy raged across the continent, well-fed by articles supplied by the playwright. Ionesco wrote, "If my failures continue on this scale I will certainly be a success." [22]

CHAPTER 4

The Second Series of Anti-Plays

> "Everything is nothing but contradiction."

I *Jack or the Submission*—"I adore hashed brown potatoes!"

JACK or The Submission (*Jacques ou la soumission*, 1955), which Ionesco termed a naturalistic comedy, and its sequel, *The Future Is in Eggs or It Takes All Sorts to Make a World* (*L'Avenir est dans les oeufs ou il faut de tout pour faire un monde*, 1957), are hilarious parodies of domestic drama in which, according to Ionesco, with his accustomed flair for a serious joke, "both the language and behavior of the characters are noble and distinguished. But this language gets dislocated and disintegrates." [1] The noble and distinguished behavior is Ionesco's caustic reference to how people act in the confined world of accepted morality. The characters in these two plays exaggerate usually expected responses into a nightmare of surrealist fantasy in which their behavior becomes a new naturalism of total disorder.

An unwilling Jack finally gives in, performs his duty, submits to the pressure of his family to "adore hashed brown potatoes," then to marry, and finally to produce children. Ionesco had written that he chose to write plays about "nothing, rather than about secondary problems (social, political, sexual, etc.)." [2] These two plays are all about sex, but sex mechanized, clowned, devoid of life-giving communication. The mystery and promise of emotional impulses are subjected to convention and decree, transformed into logical commodities.

"All of the characters, except Jack, could wear masks," it is noted in the stage directions, for they are totally dehumanized. Father, mother, sister, and grandparents gather around the hero,

who is "sprawled on the equally sprawled armchair," [3] and plead
with him to change his attitude. Mother Jack recites the hack-
neyed list of a mother's sacrifices. "I let your diapers dry on you.
. . . It was I . . . who gave you your first spankings. . . . I
have been more than a mother to you, I've been a true sweetheart,
a husband, a sailor, a buddy, a goose." [4] Father Jack denounces
him as "no son of mine" and threatens to leave. "I'll pack my bags
and you'll never see me again except at mealtimes and sometimes
during the day and in the night to get a bite to eat." [5] Grandfather
Jack and Grandmother Jack add their octogenarian squeaks but
Jack remains obstinately silent. Sister Jacqueline, who has called
him an example of "the obnubilation of puberty," is given the
private responsibility of reaching Jack. She does so in twenty-
seven words concentrated, "according to their gender," in the
"three" words, "chronometrable."

The nonsense syllables repeat the device of the earlier plays:
random sounds and coined words uttered with utmost seriousness
become weapons of tyranny. "Oh words, what crimes are committed in your name!" Jack cries, but he succumbs and says what all
have been waiting to hear, "Oh well, yes, yes, na, I adore hashed
brown potatoes!" which he repeats with less and less enthusiasm.
This seemingly innocuous submission has opened the door to
total disintegration. Like the Pupil he becomes a victim of language. He must now submit to marriage, a contractually prear-
ranged liaison with Roberta I, who enters in bridal gown and veil
accompanied by Father Robert and Mother Robert. The catalogue of the young girl's attractions is recited. She has feet, arm-
pits, thighs, hips and "green pimples on her beige skin, red breasts
on a mauve background, an illuminated navel, a tongue the color
of tomato sauce, pan-browned square shoulders, and all the meat
needed to merit the highest commendation." [6]

The surrealistic combination of colors and gastronomic delights
excites the family sexually, but Jack is unimpressed. When the veil
is lifted Roberta is shown as having two noses. Jack wants one
with three noses. This does not deter Father Robert, who takes his
daughter out and returns with his "second only daughter." Roberta II, played by the same actress, enters with the preferred
three noses. Jack, still struggling to maintain some semblance of

resistance and to preserve his individuality, makes no romantic overtures. The onlookers are furious. Father Jack accuses his ungrateful son of having lied, of never having adored hashed brown potatoes. Horrified, they all leave, but remain behind the doors to spy on the bewildering, grotesque seduction scene which follows.

Roberta II, first timidly then with greater assurance, calling herself "the joy of living, of dying," breaks down Jack's last defenses. She tells a macabre tale of dream images in which a guinea pig giving birth produces cancer. Jack responds with a counterstory of his birth at fourteen years of age, how he had refused to accept the situation. The courtship consists of these two stories, sounds and words used as emotional enticement. Jack ends his tale by saying, "Anything is preferable to my present situation. Even a new one." [7]

Roberta II, now in full swing, ready to ensnare her mate, shifts to a declamatory style as her flow of words gathers momentum. She tells of horses and the miller who killed his child, his wife and himself, the stallion and mares whinnying, galloping, bursting into flames. The erotic symbols culminate with Roberta II's open invitation to plunge down and dissolve "in my locks which drizzle . . . rain. My mouth trickles down, . . . the sky trickles down, the stars run, trickle down, trickle." [8] Language having been exhausted, the two lovers shift to rapid nonsense syllables at Roberta's suggestion that all that is needed for total communication is one word, "cat," which she uses to express all events and emotions, for, she says, "It's easier to talk that way." In their rising ecstasy, Roberta II reveals her hand, which has nine fingers. Jack is elated: "You're rich, I'll marry you."

The others enter, circling the lovers in a lewd dance as Roberta II and Jack squirm in sexual embraces. All become animals croaking and groaning in the darkness, performing a ritual celebration of entrance into marriage. Roberta II, the combination of destruction and creation, of gaiety and sorrow, of ruin and peace, squats on the floor in victory, her three noses quivering and "her nine fingers moving like snakes." [9]

II   *The Future Is in Eggs*—"You're neglecting
production! . . . It's your duty!"

The sequel, *The Future Is in Eggs*, begins three years later with
Roberta II and Jack in the same squatting position as at the end
of *The Submission*, purring the word "cat" and deeply involved in
sexual embraces. The families are upset, for the lovers have neglected production. "Nothing happens," says Father Jack. "We
must get some results quickly!" "Why don't you get on with it?
After all, it is your main duty," chortles Jacqueline, and the
parents and grandparents echo in choral support, "It's your duty!"
—the same cries as in *Victims of Duty*. Marriage must result in
the continuation of the race, the white race, the birth of more Jacks
and Robertas, of hideous, senseless mechanical puppets.

Production is the key word of modern civilization. To the accompaniment of group endorsement, the two lovers perform their
duty. Baskets of eggs are brought in and Jack is placed on the
hatching table surrounded by a mountain of eggs. The tumultuous
scene rises in intensity, the onlookers calling for more production,
more eggs. Mother Jack thinks of the future, of what careers the
offspring shall pursue. Suggestions fly from everyone in rapid succession. Among other things, the children shall be bankers, pigs,
policemen, opportunists, leeks and onions, cannon fodder, and
omelettes. "As it was in the past, the future lies in eggs!" are the
final words of the deceased and revived Grandfather Jack. Young
Jack, however, still retains a touch of rebellion. He calls for the
progeny to be pessimists, anarchists, and nihilists, and casts a
nostalgic look at the glorious past. "I want a fountain of light,
incandescent water, fire of ice, snows of fire," he cries, just before
the stage collapses in utter darkness.

The two Jack plays are weird, surrealist extensions of the boulevard drama of love and sex. The basic ingredients, romantic
courtship, mating, and child bearing, are reduced to their ultimate
essence until they are deprived of all meaning, the family drama
is transformed into a grotesque parade of seemingly noble and
distinguished middle class characters who become mechanical
symbols. The free play of the imagination replaces logical and
psychological interrelationships.

III　*The New Tenant*—"Be careful, be careful of my circles."

In *The New Tenant* (*Le Nouveau Locataire*, 1953) a single metaphor is again expanded, but this time more directly, cumulatively, and terrifyingly, with less reliance on verbal nonsense and non sequiturs. As in the other early short pieces, the characters are noncharacters, elements in the playing out of a visual explanation of an idea. Things, in this case furniture, take their revenge. The eggs of Jack's submission to copulation and production now become sofas, paintings, chairs, tables, which envelop the stage, completely encircling the tenant: a sight gag is transformed into a hideous joke. Jimmy Durante, the comedian, once had a comparable nightclub sketch in which the word "wood" is mentioned and arouses delirious enthusiasm at all that "wood" implies. To the accompaniment of song and dance, all kinds of wood objects are brought in and piled onstage, from canes to pianos to a final triumphant outhouse, with the comedian buried under the mountain of objects. Ionesco uses the same heightened, increased tension as the furniture mounts higher and higher, occupying all available space. The underlying spirit, however, is not that of a vaudeville routine, but of a deadly serious social comment. Behind the accumulation of objects, completely removed from communication with others or any contact with the outside world, is a man who has found a safe place where he can be at home. Pinter later used the same device of the cluttered room as a haven from outside fears, a symbolic return to the womb, in such plays as *The Caretaker*. Material accumulation is the preoccupation of modern man. The new tenant, a grotesque representative of contemporary living, is buried under things.

The play opens in silence in a bare room with large doors on each side. The female caretaker enters singing and looks out the open window. The man who is to occupy the room, a middle-aged gentleman in a bowler hat and striped trousers, comes in unexpectedly, measures the room precisely, and stands like a figure of death: cold, silent, removed. The shabby caretaker, speaking with an Irish accent, lets loose a flood of words without pause, garrulously recounting past events in her life, notes on the former occupants of the room, and her willingness to be of service—the stereotype of the talkative landlady. The new tenant resents the flood of words and orders her to close the window and to leave. "I really shan't be needing your services. . . . I shall be looking after myself, you see." [10] Furious at being dismissed, she exits as two moving men start placing furniture in the exact places indicated by the tenant. He traces a chalk circle around an armchair and a chest of books in the middle of the room, the protective center for his own occupancy. Through both doors the furniture comes: lamps, screens, sofas, paintings. When all floor space is occupied, ladders are used to pile objects higher and higher, up to and through the ceiling in a "ponderous ballet," with the Furniture Movers, slow-moving but insistent, and the Gentleman "in ever-diminishing space." A radio, the only possible means of reaching beyond the enclosure, is placed near the armchair and approved by the Gentleman because it does not work. When the room is completely occupied the furniture still keeps on coming. The stairway up to the sixth floor is jammed, traffic has "come to a standstill in the streets," the subway lines are blocked, and even the Thames River has been dammed up. The tenant is now invisible, hidden behind a wall of furniture. As the Furniture Movers manage to scramble up and over the mountain of articles, the Gentleman's last order is to turn out the lights and the stage is left in utter darkness.

Things have replaced people. The tenant is beyond communication. He has no need to communicate. This short play is a theatrical and visual experience, not literature. Ionesco works in stage images which have their own dramatic power. *The New Tenant* is not as suggestive as *The Chairs* or *The Bald Soprano,* nor is it as wildly imaginative as *Jack;* but it is a relentlessly repetitive demonstration of death in life, of the triumph of total isolation, a depressing portrayal of non-human existence.

IV   *Victims of Duty*—"Personality doesn't exist."

Ionesco was amused by the contradictory comments that greeted his work. He was called a serious writer, a master of amusing jokes, a humorless man, a mystic, a realist, "a violent critic of contemporary society," and a writer who had failed "to denounce an unjust world." [11] *The Lesson,* about a sadistic professor who kills his pupils, was regarded as highly amusing. *The Chairs,* in which two old people assume that empty chairs are creatures of flesh, was thought to be an entertaining joke. Why not then be a joker? Ionesco wrote *Seven Short Sketches,* which included *The Motor Show* and *Maid to Marry,* intended as "jokes" but hailed as examples of serious abstract drama. To eliminate all possible misunderstanding he decided he would write not a comedy, or a drama, or a tragedy, but simply a lyrical text, something "lived." "I transferred to the stage my doubts and my deepest despairs and turned them into dialogue; gave flesh and blood to my inner conflicts, wrote with the greatest sincerity and tore at my entrails. I entitled this 'Victims of Duty.' " [12]

Victims of Duty (*Victimes du devoir,* 1953) is the most complex of the early plays, a pseudo-drama of which Ionesco was particularly fond. The multiple themes and technical devices are combined in a highly orchestrated travesty of detective stories, Freudian drama, and Ionesco's own work. The opening scene discovers Choubert reading a newspaper while Madeleine, his wife, is darning socks, another scene with a middle-aged married couple, similar to the opening of *The Bald Soprano.* Madeleine asks if there is any news in the paper and Choubert's reply is typical of Ionesco's approach to a senseless world in which all events are of equal importance. He tells of cosmic disturbances, the neighbors being fined for letting the dog dirty the pavement, and the dream regrets of another age. "Nowadays men have lost the peace of mind they had in the past." [13]

The ensuing dialogue is logical and coherent, covering politics, literature, and attacks on Bertolt Brecht's theory of alienation. All citizens, Choubert reads, are being urged to cultivate detachment, "our last hope of finding an answer to the economic crisis, the confusion of the spirit and the problems of existence." [14] The plea for detachment is a government suggestion that Choubert fears may become an official decree, and everyone who is law-abiding will have to do his duty. The major theme is sounded. Obedience to duty as decreed by law, moral or political, leads to the destruction of individuality and the senseless deterioration of the self. Each topic of conversation ends in abrupt silence, a device for shifting to the next topic, which may be fairly unrelated to what has gone before but does refer to the general overall examination of "duty." Choubert discusses the theatre. All plays since the Greeks, he maintains, are actually detective stories. "The police arrive, there's an investigation and the criminal is unmasked." Madeleine suggests that this original idea be brought to the attention of the experts such as "the Professors at the *Collège de France,* the influential members of the Agricultural School, the Norwegians or some of those veterinary surgeons," [15] all of whom have ideas and are certainly no less qualified than the drama critics.

A young detective, polite and well-dressed, "a nice man you feel you can trust," knocks on the door. He is seeking the correct spelling of the name of the previous tenant: was it "Mallot, with a t at the end, or Mallod with a d?" The interrogation which follows is a Kafkaesque ordeal in which the realistic domestic opening scene is transformed into a witch's sabbath and the ultimate dismemberment of Choubert. The apologetic Detective orders Choubert, who did not know Mallot but is trying to be helpful, to explore his memory, to go down into his subconscious to find Mallot with a "t." As Choubert digs deeply into his past, time vanishes, reality and fantasy intermingle. The Detective assumes control, becoming the father figure as Madeleine becomes the mother and mistress in his dream sequence. In a return to childhood, Choubert relives a ritual of sacrifice, penitence, and hope. He crawls through tunnels, under the table, around the furniture, climbs high mountains, getting up on chairs in a dazed hypnotic trance. Madeleine appears in a low-cut gown and acts out an erotic scene with her husband, her words like those of the Professor in *The Lesson* or Roberta II in *The Future Is in Eggs,* a jungle of sensual sounds: "a step . . . a stair . . . la, la, la, la." [16] Deeper, deeper, further down, wallowing in mud, Choubert follows the demands of the Detective, his responses an unfolding of sexual impulses.

As the dream vanishes, Madeleine appears once again, old and decrepit, the golden past now the ugliness of the present. Choubert takes her hand, wondering about their lost youth. "Love never dies. . . . Who made you old like that? . . . Oh, if only we could go singing and skipping and jumping again!" [17] She rejects any tenderness, trapped in the female resentment of sexual submission, "Our love in the night, our love in the mud." Madeleine and the Detective act out the marital quarrels of the mother-father stereotypes. Choubert is told he is a product of Cartesian logic. "You would never have been here, were it not for that endless chain of cause and effect, . . . for everything in the universe is the result of a whole system of causation, not excepting you." [18]

The search for Mallot in the recesses of his memory continues, for it is now the Detective reminds him, "a question of life and death. It's your duty. The fate of all mankind depends on you." [19] Choubert climbs higher, crossing mountains, wading through snow and ice, flying through space. After a quick blackout, the lights come up on Choubert sprawled in the wastepaper basket with the Detective and Madeleine standing over him. A mysterious Lady appears in the background, silently watching. Madeleine brings in coffee cups until they pile high on the cupboard, an accumulation of things, similar to the furniture in *The New Tenant*. A tall, bearded, disheveled poet, Nicolas D'Eu, enters as the Detective, to fill in the gaps still left in Choubert's memory, orders him to eat a huge loaf of bread that he has taken from his suitcase. As the bread is stuffed into Choubert's mouth, the Poet resumes the earlier discussion on the nature of drama: "We'll get rid of the principle of identity and unity of character and let movement and dynamic psychology take its place . . . We are not ourselves . . . personality doesn't exist," [20] a summary of Ionesco's own approach to the theatre. The Detective is more conventional: "As for me I remain Aristotelically logical, true to myself, faithful to my duty and full of respect for my bosses . . . I don't believe in the absurd, everything hangs together, everything can be comprehended in time." [21] Nicolas is infuriated at the recital of the rules of realism, denies he is a poet, spurns the literary life, and adds, "We've got Ionesco and Ionesco, that's enough!" He assumes control of the situation, calls the Detective mad, and stabs him with a knife, the victimizer now the victim. The Detective dies exclaiming, "I am . . . a victim . . . of duty!" Nicolas now orders Choubert to eat the loaf of bread as they all echo the Detective's last words, that they too are victims of duty. Ending the play, they join in a choral chant of "Chew! Swallow! Chew! Swallow!" The Lady, who until now has not said a word, accompanies them. Wallowing in the mysterious has become an act of physical survival, the restoration of memory, dependent on stuffing bread down one's throat. Mallot with a "t" or a "d" hasn't been discovered. The tyrant is either the Detective or the Poet. Choubert, like Jack and the Pupil, has been completely destroyed. His calm, uneventful life has been lifted for a moment into adventure and fancy and then thrust back into total submission, as a mournful example of compliance with duty.

V *Improvisation*—"If something is falsely false,
it's also truly true."

Most of the other short plays are exercises in developing a style. *The Motor Show* (*Le Salon de l'automobile*) is a fearful glance at sales promotion. *Foursome* (*Scène à quatre*) has three ridiculous louts wooing a woman at the same time and tearing her to bits. *The Hard Boiled Egg* (*L'oeuf dur*) is a pseudo-ballet on gourmet cooking. *The Picture* (*Le Tableau*) has a doleful artist who is trying to sell a painting end up buying the canvas of the expected patron. In *Maid to Marry* (*La Jeune fille à marier*) a mother discusses her daughter with an eligible suitor, but the Maid turns out to be a husky-voiced, well-bred girl of ninety-three who "owes us eighty years, so that makes her only thirteen." In *Frenzy for Two, or More* (*Délire à deux*) a couple married seventeen years engage in a heated, meaningless quarrel while a war goes on outside and a wounded soldier appears surrounded by bodiless heads and headless bodies. In *The Leader* (*Le Maître*) the character of the title finally appears to his admirers, but he is lacking a head. This seems to them of little importance, since a true leader doesn't need a head. *Salutations* (*Les Salutations*) is a long catalogue of the various ways of responding to the greeting, "How are you?" and ends at the height of a babbling brawl with the line, "We're getting on ionescoically!"

Most worthy of extended comment is *Improvisation or The Shepherd's Chameleon* (*L'Impromptu de l'Alma*, 1956), in which critics and professional commentators, including Ionesco, are subjected to ridicule. Instead of writing a literary essay, Ionesco wrote theatrical dialogue. Bartholomeus I, II, and III, dressed in academic robes, drop in on Ionesco as he is snoring at his desk.

The scholars, critics all, do most of the talking, bombarding the playwright with advice, suggestions, rules, and regulations. They discuss alienation, existentialism, and Ionesco's new play, which is the same play as *Improvisation,* constantly contradicting one another. Ionesco protests, "I find you're expressing yourself in a very contradictory way. I'm all for contradiction, everything is nothing but contradiction." [22]

The scholars ignore Ionesco, claiming that he doesn't know that opposites are identical. Bartholomeus I says, "When I say that something is truly true, that means that it's falsely false," to which Bartholomeus II says, "Or just the reverse: if something is falsely false, it's also truly true." Ionesco replies, "I'd never have thought of that. Oh, how clever you are!"

The scholars overwhelm Ionesco with their syllogisms, platitudes, insults, and directives. He finally gathers his courage and makes one long, serious speech, summarizing his own approach to art.

I blame these doctors for discovering elementary truths and dressing them up in exaggerated language so that these elementary truths appear to have gone mad. These truths, however, like all truths, even elementary ones, are open to argument. . . . For my part I believe sincerely in the poverty of the poor, I deplore it, but it is true and can serve as material for the theatre; I also believe in the grave cares and anxieties that may beset the rich; but in my case it is neither from the wretchedness of the poor nor the unhappiness of the rich that I draw the substance of my drama.[23]

The long declamation ends with the basic philosophy of Ionesco that "these hidden desires, these dreams, these secret conflicts . . . are the source of all our actions and of the reality of history." He is wound up, taking himself seriously, ready to continue lecturing on the nature of life. The Maid comes over and places a scholar's gown on him. Ionesco has become an academician, and has fallen into his own trap. *Improvisation* is a long-winded and somewhat tiresome debate with an appeal to audiences more interested in literary games than theatrical magic, but it serves well as a comment on Ionesco by the playwright himself.

CHAPTER 5

Amédée and The Killer

> "Oh, God! There's nothing we can do!"
>
> (*The Killer*)

AFTER the intial series of one-act plays, all produced in little avant-garde theatres, Ionesco explored the full length drama with *Amédée*. It did not prove to be a popular success, and he abandoned the longer form until *The Killer* a few years later, which launched the series of major works which occupied his attention for the next decade.

I   *Amédée*—"Love . . . puts everything right."

Amédée or How to Get Rid of It, (*Amédée ou comment s'en debarrasser*, 1954) is about an unhappy married couple and a growing corpse which occupies their living quarters. In his accustomed ambivalent manner, Ionesco wrote, "In 'Amédée' I am dealing again with a couple. What is important for me and what gives the play meaning is the corpse. . . . The corpse is . . . original sin. The growing corpse is time." [1] As the play opens, Amédée, a middle-aged bourgeois playwright, sits at his desk waiting for an inspired sentence. He has been doing the same thing for fifteen years and only two sentences have come in all that time, ever since that strange being in the next room has been with them. Madeleine, his wife, a sharp-tongued shrew, bitterly regales her husband with insults and pleas of self-pity. Madeleine, with the same name as the scolding wife in *Victims of Duty*, gives the orders, makes the demands, runs the household, earns the money. Amédée does the household chores, answers the doorbell, lowers the basket to bring up food, and listens to Madeleine's endless nagging. They have lived this way, isolated, shut up in the dismal flat, "all because of him," the figure lying in the bedroom, and now mushrooms are beginning to grow in the dark corners of their flat.

When the clock strikes nine, Madeleine puts on her hat and goes to the office, a telephone switchboard in one corner of the room. Three conversations go on simultaneously, her business calls, the continuing conversation with Amédée, and his calls to the vendor in the street below, so that lines are an alternate mixture of "cream cheese," "countersigned by the Chief Constable," and "You've forgotten the leeks." When the clock strikes twelve Madeleine takes off her hat and joins Amédée for lunch. The two levels of dialogue that now play against each other refer to the growing object next door and Madeleine's constant wails of self pity, so that "What have I ever done to deserve this," is followed by "You've forgotten to close the eyelids again!"

A voice from outside interrupts the conversation. Knocking on the door or the ringing of bells or outside sounds generate a sense of fear of the unknown invading the secure area of the room. The Postman comes with a letter for Amédée at 29, Generals Road, which he refuses to accept: "There's more than one number 29, Generals Road, there's more than one Generals Road, there are lots of them." The same words are repeated as though they expressed a totally different thought, the obvious truism which is equally false.

The mushrooms grow larger. The noises in the next room grow louder. Finally the mystery of what is in the next room is solved when enormous feet come sliding through the open door, part of a corpse that is growing in "geometrical progression," described as "the incurable disease of the dead." Since to Ionesco all drama is basically a detective story, he employs the devices of increased evidence, uncertainty as to the evil-doer, and eventual revelation of the criminal; but the usual straight narrative of police plots is turned and twisted into surrealistic shape, adding to the logic of the criminal investigator, the illogic of the dreamer.

Now that the mystery in *Amédée* is solved the problem is a more immediate domestic one, what to do with a corpse that threatens to occupy all the living space. When the action resumes a few hours later in the second act, the corpse has taken over most of the stage and is visibly growing before our eyes. The feet jerk forward, giving Amédée and Madeleine a violent shock on each occasion. Amédée measures the distance covered: "Six inches in twenty minutes." The mushrooms are now giant size, sprouting against the wall. Ionesco had written that the play could "not be condemned for being untrue to life for mushrooms grow on stage, which is incontrovertible proof that the mushrooms are real mushrooms." [2]

As the body keeps moving, Madeleine and Amédée discuss how it got there. They are not clear whether it was a lover of Madeleine or a baby that they were taking care of, or someone they had murdered. They cannot recall the past as "dreams and real life, memories and imagination" become interwoven. Madeleine is the more practical one. She says, "Whether this old man's really the baby or the young lover doesn't alter the situation. And you've got to get us out of it." [3] They decide to remove the body that night. As the corpse and mushrooms grow larger, Madeleine resumes her knitting as Amédée collapses into the armchair, exhausted.

A dream sequence follows as Amédée's memory explores the past, seeking the time when the hope of happiness was possible, before a corpse possessed their life. Amédée II and Madeleine II appear as young lovers on their wedding night. For Amédée it is the moment of radiant light and shimmering hopes, but Madeleine was then as she is now: vicious, unyielding, the guilty partner who murders love. Women do not fare well in Ionesco's plays. Madeleine in *Victims of Duty* watches with sadistic pleasure as her husband is cruelly tortured. The Madeleine of *Amédée* never permits a joyous embrace. To Ionesco, love and sex as a means of communication, of touching and reaching out to the other person, of openings on to the mystery of life, are the victims of marriage by contractual arrangement and conventional convenience. In such marriages the irrational aspect of love is controlled, channeled and eventually crushed. Madeleine in *Victims of Duty* or in *Amédée* destroys love, throttling its vibrant, self-fulfilling vitality.

Amédée calls tenderly to his young bride and she responds by saying, "Don't touch me. You sting, sting, sting. You hu-urt me!" [4] She fears bodily contact, and uses the serpent sounds to empha-

size the pain and physical discomfort of sex. Abandoning the communication of love, the only communication she has left is hate
and constant bickering. Amédée talks of the dawning spring,
rooms filled with sunshine, a glorious light, the repeated Lost Paradise images of "snow on mountains," "limpid lakes and green
forests." Madeleine's hoarse, jarring, antiphonal response is fearful
death images of bayonets and machine guns, of darkness and
forests of slime. He tries to reach her with the call of "Madeleine,
darling," and she answers caustically, "Amédée, wretch!" He tries
to build love anew, to start all over again. "We are happy. In a
house of glass." She retorts, "A house of brass," and the words
"brass and glass," "light and night" ring back and forth until the
figures fade and the older couple is once more sitting in the living
room surrounded by the corpse and growing mushrooms. To the
accompaniment of music and shifting green lights contrasting the
beauty of Amédée's faith in love, which "puts everything right,"
and the ugliness of Madeleine's response, the ballet of removing
the body ensues. Bit by bit, across the room, through the windows, the huge body, then the hands, and finally the head are
pushed out onto the street below.

The third act takes place in the public square below the window, a reverse shot of the previous interior scene. An American
soldier thrown out of a bar sees Amédée pulling the huge body
towards the river and offers to help him. They both tug manfully
but too strongly. The noise arouses the dogs, sets the trains in
motion, and brings on the police, who chase Amédée around the
corpse as the bystanders urge them on. The dead man lifts
Amédée high above the crowd, beyond the reach of his pursuers,
a grotesque occurrence which everyone onstage takes quite naturally. Amédée flies out into space, a device which was worked out
more fully in *Pedestrian of the Air*. He returns to drop a shoe or
say a few words to the onlookers below. "I don't want to get carried away . . . I'm all for progress . . . I believe in social realism." [5] But it is of no avail. Off he goes, Madeleine shouting after
him the tasteless line, "You may have gone up in the world, but
you are not going up in *my* estimation!" [6] The police leave, the
customers return to the bar, the future of the body or Amédée is

unknown, as a woman in an upstairs room says, "Let's close the shutter, . . . the show's over."

Ionesco wrote an alternate ending to the play to avoid some of the technical difficulties. As the lights change in the living room at the end of the dance sequence, all the characters of the final scene appear from out of the darkness and the room becomes outside space without the need to change the set. This first full-length play of Ionesco is an overextended metaphor stretched out beyond endurable length. The slow expansion of the corpse until it overwhelms the stage, surrounded by enormous poisonous mushrooms, is an overdrawn surrealist image. In contrast, the chairs that fill all space in *The Chairs* are essential to the suicide of the couple deserting the awaiting public. The shorter length provided for dramatic intensity and artistic control. Ionesco, not too happy with the reception the play received, returned to the one-act form with which he had been more successful. Yet despite its wearisome length, *Amédée* is an excellent example of the themes and devices of Ionesco—frustrated marriage, love turned barren in a rational world, the desire to return to a Utopian past, the equally contradictory nature of all events, and, in the symbolic figure of the corpse, the victory of the dead. With his usual deceptive innocence, Ionesco denied that the play had any symbolic meaning. "It tells us an ordinary story," he wrote, "that could have happened to a great many of us. It is a slice of life, a realistic play." [7]

II   *The Killer*—"I do so need another life."

Five years later Ionesco returned to the full-length play. The lessons of *Amédée* were well learned. *The Killer* (*Tueur sans gages*, 1959) is a major achievement, displaying full mastery of a developed style and an increased awareness of theatrical possibility. The shorter form was abandoned and in succession followed *Rhinoceros, Exit the King, Pedestrian of the Air, Hunger and Thirst,* and *Massacre Games,* establishing Ionesco as a playwright with a comprehensive body of work covering twenty years of creative activity.

The Killer is a landmark in the Theatre of the Irrational. The stage is no longer a visual demonstration of an expanded single image, but a many-sided presentation in grotesque and fanciful scenes of the search for a different reality. The plot has a definite progression; a broad canvas involves a wide range of characters; hilarious nonsense is incorporated as a contributing factor without dominating the sequence of events; and the overall pessimism results as a failure of ill-equipped man to find a reasonable explanation for the existence of evil in a rational world.

The basic story is simple. Bérenger, the name Ionesco uses for his protagonist in the next three plays, is an average middle-aged citizen who visits the Radiant City and discovers behind the facade of beauty and light the fear and terror of an unknown Killer. He avoids involvement, but when his dream fiancée is slain, he sets out to investigate the crime. In an amazing confrontation scene he finally faces the Killer and goes down to defeat with the despairing final line "Oh God! There's nothing we can do. . . . What can we do. . . . What can we do . . ." The simple story, however, is worked out with Ionesco in full control of his special devices, which he plays one against another in a rich orchestration of non-Aristotelian theatre.

The scene opens on an empty stage bathed in blue and white light to create the impression of peace and quiet. Bérenger enters with the Architect, who is his guide on a tour of the Radiant City. He is overjoyed by the incredible miracle, that beyond dreary urban filth there is a place of sunny streets with grass and "rose-pink flowers." The Architect assures him that every item has been carefully planned, "Nothing was to be left to chance," [8] even the weather is perfect. Bérenger, with the impetus supplied by this undreamed-of outer reality, rediscovers his inner self, thanks to the power of modern technology and scientific planning. While the Architect answers mysterious phone calls from a telephone in his pocket, Bérenger in an ecstatic mood says, "It's quite wrong to talk of a world within and a world without, as separate worlds; there's an initial impulse, of course, which starts from us, and when it can't project itself, when it can't fulfill itself, when there's not total agreement between the inner me and the outer me, then it's a catastrophe." [9] The unconscious longings of man, distorted and warped by the ugliness of living, are kept alive by the continuing beauty of hidden dreams. For Bérenger the "sickness of living" has been replaced by indescribable bliss, by the incomparable brilliance of the sunlit city. The forgotten light has been restored. Inner needs and external reality are in harmony. "Yours is the right system, your methods are rational," [10] he tells the Architect.

The claims of modern technology to enhance the quality of life, to make dreams actuality, have been given tangible proof. The Architect understands little of what Bérenger is saying. He is too busy talking on the telephone to his secretary, who is thinking of leaving her job, and he is insensitive to philosophic speculation; but he does manage to drop a hint to Bérenger that "reality unlike dreams, can turn into a nightmare." Bérenger feels alive and young and calls out "Mademoiselle, will you marry me?" as the blonde secretary, Mademoiselle Dany enters. The Architect discusses business with her and she replies mechanically, "Yes, Monsieur," which Bérenger assumes to be the answer to his proposal. Ionesco again uses the device of simultaneous conversations. Bérenger is able to love again, like Amédée of the dream sequence. He is a man newly inspired. He will buy a house in the Radiant City where he and Mademoiselle Dany can live in happiness. "I do so need another life." Before Bérenger can receive a definite response, Mademoiselle Dany quits her job despite the Architect's warning that he can no longer be held responsible for her protection. The lights dim, becoming gray and foreboding. Suddenly, stones are thrown, windows are shut, sounds of broken glass are heard, and then a shot. The Architect bluntly tells Bérenger that the people who live in this district want to leave because every day several bodies are found in the pool, murdered by an unknown elusive stranger. Bérenger's ideals are shattered. "There are no radiant districts." He feels tired, cold, ill, and once again in despair at the sickness of life.

The Architect, who turns out to be also the superintendent of police, takes Bérenger to a neighborhood bistro and explains the history of the Killer. Victims are lured to the edge of the pool, shown obscene photos and a picture of the Colonel, then hit over the head and left to drown. Ionesco's original short story on which the play is based was entitled "The Colonel's Photo." As they sit at the table talking, the news arrives that Mademoiselle Dany has been drowned. Bérenger runs off shouting, "This can't go on! We must *do* something!"

The glorious technical achievement of the modern city had ignored the human factor. Geometry and cement and calculators have constructed the appearance of beauty, but the dark, mysterious, uncontrollable fears have not been eliminated. Mademoiselle Dany, who resisted the anonymity which surrounded her, sought freedom from the established machine and has become the latest victim of the dread Killer.

The simple bright colors of Act One give way in Act Two to the heavy, drab furniture of Bérenger's ground-floor apartment. Edouard, thin, sickly, formally dressed, is sitting in an armchair. Through the windows can be seen and heard the life of the ugly district, the people passing by, the heavy traffic, children shouting, radios playing from the upper floors, the house elevator moving up and down, the rasping conversation of the prying female Concierge. Act Two is the weakest section of the play, an interlude before the mounting confusion and disaster of the final act. It is devoted mainly to the failure to recognize evil when it is present even among one's own associates. Edouard's briefcase flies open and the contents fall over the table and floor, an amazing accumulation of things, a minor repetition of the furniture in *The New Tenant* or the cups in *Victims of Duty*. The items in the briefcase are incriminating evidence: the Colonel's photo, obscene pictures, lists of intended victims. Bérenger has no intention of accusing Edouard. He has neither the wit nor the acuity. They both dash out to turn the material over to the police and in the confusion leave the briefcase behind. Bérenger's naive insistence on pursuing the Killer finds him unable to discover evidence in his own immediate surroundings and insensitive to the complicity of all in evil.

III   *Mother Peep's Geese*—"Fair shares for all. I'll keep
       the lion's share for myself and my geese."

In a marvelous mélange of shifting scenes, the final section presents the obstacles in Bérenger's path to achieve justice and ends with the memorable and obligatory confrontation with the Killer. A raised pavement with a railing along the edge occupies the rear part of the stage. Above and behind the wall the varied activities of a busy boulevard take place. On the steps leading downstage, Bérenger continues his search for the briefcase. These two levels provide the opportunity for simultaneous activities which are apparently independent but which interrelate since the problem of social health affects all.

At the outset on the upper level the Concierge, who is now Mother Peep, is addressing a crowd, urging them to serve under her banner of the white goose. "Me and my geese are asking for power," she pleads in a parody of early Nazi appeals to the people. The conversation of Bérenger and Edouard in the foreground is interlarded with Mother Peep's lines and the shouts of the crowd. Despite his protestations that his plays are nonpolitical, Ionesco's Mother Peep scene is a devastating attack on totalitarianism. Rarely has language been used more adroitly to expose the total emptiness of political sloganeering. Mother Peep, her back to the audience, her head above the railing, her geese-banners flying, promises an end to mystification but "to demystify, you need a new mystification." She will change everything, which means changing nothing. Mankind will be "disalienated," but first "we must alienate each individual man," and of course each slogan ends with the recurring refrain, "soup kitchens for all." The contradictions multiply, the opposite of each statement is a return to the original statement. Peep will be "para-scientific," objectivity will be subjective, stupidity will become intelligence, war will be declared peace, and the intellectuals be forced to do the goose step. Bérenger's discovery that the briefcase is not with him and his frantic calls to Edouard in his desperate yearning to reach the Police are all sandwiched in between the loud shouts of acclaim and the marching beat of the goose step. The transformation of all values, the regimentation of unresisting geese, forms the antiphonal chant to Bérenger's search for justice.

A Man carrying an identical black briefcase interspersing his remarks with drinks from a bottle, is the lone voice raised against Mother Peep's mass hysteria. He calls for a hero who "dares to think against history." An Old Man with an umbrella and another identical black briefcase enters seeking directions to the Danube even though he is in Paris. Mother Peep, to increasing applause of

the multitude, calls for replacing old myths with new platitudes
"Fair shares for all. I'll keep the lion's share for myself and my
geese." The Man shouts "Down with Mother Peep!" and argues
that political revolutions accomplish nothing, that economics will
take care of itself, that the scientists and artists are the only true
revolutionaries. A wild melee ensues. Edouard and Bérenger are
pulling briefcases, passing them from hand to hand, the Old Man
keeps asking for directions to the Danube, and Mother Peep with
another briefcase in her hand, hits the Man over the head, silenc-
ing the sole opposition voice. She disappears behind the parapet,
her hideous face reappearing for a final reminder, "My geese have
liquidated him. But only physically." [11] Briefcases open, the contents flying all over the stage. The Man's briefcase is full of wine
bottles, Mother Peep's is full of cardboard boxes of the goose
game, and what is in the Old Man's briefcase is never known.

Edouard is sent back to the room to recover his own briefcase.
Bérenger decides to move on alone to the Prefecture of Police.
The parapet is now filled with gendarmes and soldiers. Army
trucks roll by, sirens are heard, and police whistles screech.
Bérenger tries to fight his way through but is caught in the traffic
jam, on his important humanitarian mission. He is stopped by a
tall Policeman who looks like the Architect, is cross-examined,
asked for identification, and detained. The upholders of the law
prevent Bérenger from bringing the law to fulfill its function. Bu-
reaucracy, stupidity, regulations deter action. The scene suddenly
changes. The wall in the rear disappears and Bérenger is on a
long, winding, deserted street with the Prefecture buildings in the
distant background. He is alone surrounded by an eerie silence.
He walks and walks and walks, getting more distraught and ap-
prehensive, trying to reach police headquarters before it is too
dark.

IV   *The Laughter of Evil*—"What good are bullets
against the resistance of an infinitely stubborn will!"

Here begins one of the longest speeches in the history of drama.
Bérenger at first talks to himself about the need to reform society
and improve the police, but above all to see that Mademoiselle
Dany's murderer is apprehended. The Killer appears, laughing

derisively. He is a small, ill-dressed man with one eye, a puny, grotesque monster. The two figures are alone in the desolate waste. Bérenger does all the talking. All the Killer does is to laugh with varying degrees of laughter, soft and cynical, loud and resolute; or he shrugs his shoulders while Bérenger, increasingly pathetic and desperate, advances every argument of conventional morality for the preservation of human values. He tries to convince the Killer that life is valuable, that men die anyway and there is no need to hasten the inevitable. He reasons that if all is vanity so is the commission of crime. He threatens the Killer physically but cannot bring himself to act. His arguments break down as he begins to take on the logic of the Killer, finding no sufficient reason why life should be preserved. As the Killer comes closer with a knife in his hand, Bérenger takes out his pistols but cannot shoot. He is reduced to total helplessness. "What good are bullets . . . against the resistance of an infinitely stubborn will!" [12] Overwhelmed by the vacuity of his own arguments, unable to convince even himself, Bérenger submits to the relentless, indomitable will of the Killer with the final cry, "Oh God! There's nothing we can do! What can we do. . . . What can we do . . ." [13]

The play is Ionesco's most pessimistic statement, his most thorough rejection of existing norms, a grim portrayal of the prevalent anomie of the rule of reason, a confirmation of the death of God and the reign of chaos. The Killer may exist only in Bérenger's imagination, a projection of the subconscious in which the man of reason faces the animal part of his nature; the final helplessness may be a recognition of the absence of valid criteria. The Killer is not a paid assassin. The French title *Tueur sans gages* implies that his services are not for hire, that he has a metaphysical existence, unavoidable, ever-present, a force that established authorities are unable to eliminate. They may be partly responsible for his continuing presence. A simple, well-intentioned Bérenger makes the effort which turns out to be his own destruction. Ionesco repeats his preoccupation with death. In *Amédée* a corpse overwhelms the living, in *The Killer* a mysterious force kills, for there is no positive force to assert life.

The dramatic techniques work effectively with the content. Characters split, merge, and coalesce. The stage is extended to encompass any space. Language varies from the multiple, incoherent conversation of the street scenes and the repetition of nonsense to the well-organized, exhausting monologue of the final debate. *The Killer* is one of Ionesco's most effective dramas.

CHAPTER 6

The Bérenger Trio

> "Escape from definitions and you will
> breathe again."
>
> *(Exit The King)*

TEN years after *The Bald Soprano* opened in a dismal Left Bank theatre to an audience of three, *Rhinoceros,* with Jean-Louis Barrault in the role of Bérenger, was presented at the Théâtre de France (formerly the Odéon) to a capacity audience of more than twelve hundred people, including André Malraux, Minister of Cultural Affairs. The Paris opening coincided with the first performance of the play in Basel, Switzerland. A few months earlier the world première had taken place at the Schauspielhaus in Düsseldorf, Germany. Orson Welles produced the play in London with Laurence Olivier as Bérenger. Productions throughout Europe and the United States followed in quick succession. The isolated and controversial avant-garde theatre of a decade earlier was now in the eager embrace of the Establishment.

In each of the three plays considered in this section, Bérenger is the central character. In *Rhinoceros* he is the meek apologetic clerk who defies totalitarian hysteria and refuses to become part of the "monstrous phenomenon of massification." [1] In *Exit The King* King Bérenger refuses to die without some insight into the meaning of death. In *Pedestrian of the Air* Bérenger, a French writer, returns from outer space with the sad report that the worlds beyond offer no better hope than man's miserable lot here. In each play Bérenger is a different person and the same person, a twentieth-century Everyman who in this triple incarnation engages death in battle to know through separate surrealist meta-

67

phors the meaning of life. None has the rich complexity of *The Killer* and all require involved technical machinery for effective staging with elaborate sound and light plots. In *Rhinoceros* herds of perissodactyls romp through the streets and Jean turns into a one-horned hoofed mammal in full view of the audience; in *Exit The King* the throne room disappears into an enveloping mist; in *Pedestrian of the Air* Bérenger walks three feet off the ground while the Sunday picnickers imitate him. By 1970 Ionesco had established a valid claim to mastery of a theatrical expression that was highly effective and distinctly original.

I *Rhinoceros*—"I'm not capitulating!"

In *The Bald Soprano* all the characters are interchangeable since none has a separate individuality. In *Rhinoceros* each of the central characters has a distinctly different response to the demands of totalitarian conformity, which requires the giving up of specific individual differences. Jean, Botard, Dudard, and Daisy become victims of rhinoceritis, a disease which consists of compliance with whatever is the norm of the moment, no matter how absurd it may be, mouthing slogans and clichés that provide acceptance. Bérenger, who almost alone of Ionesco's characters grows and changes in the course of the play, stands apart: irresolute, reluctant, but allergic to the mass epidemic, unable to respond to the pressures that surround him because something deep within him, some instinctive human need compels resistance. *Rhinoceros* is Ionesco's most human and most political play.

When the critics claimed that he had abandoned avant-garde obscurity for an obvious propaganda play, Ionesco protested that they were using his own weapons. "They formerly accused me of giving no message, now they accuse me of the exact contrary. They accused me of being incomprehensible, now they accuse me of being too clear." [2] But the play goes beyond an attack on Nazism. It lashes out at all ideologies "that lurk beneath the surface of reason" and through propaganda, emotionalism, and appeals to prejudice "transform a whole world and naturally being totalitarian, transform it totally. The play should trace and point the different stages of this phenomenon." [3]

In the opening scene Bérenger, unkempt and suffering from a

hangover, joins the highly respectable and fastidious Jean at a sidewalk café and is promptly rebuked for his appearance, his lack of self-discipline, and his failure to observe social decorum. Bérenger protests that a boring job requires a bit of relaxation on Saturday night and promises to mend his ways, to take adult education courses and go to avant-garde plays, especially those of Ionesco. Before he can pursue his re-education, the quiet Sunday morning is interrupted by the sound of a rhinoceros charging through the streets. The people in the square react quite indifferently to this violent phenomenon, explaining it away with some shallow comment as a substitute for facing its full implications. When another rhinoceros, or the same one, comes thumping and trumpeting from the opposite direction, Bérenger shows increased concern, even attacking strenuously Jean's pompous certainty as to the nature of the beast. Heated arguments ensue among the spectators as to whether the animal was a one-horned Asian or a two-horned African rhinoceros, to be resolved by a professional Logician who after a lengthy discourse on all syllogistic possibilities concludes that it was "one rhinoceros either Asiatic or African," or "one rhinoceros either African or Asiatic," or two rhinoceroses, since logically "the same creature" cannot "be born in two places at the same time." Bérenger is the only one who protests that the question has not been answered satisfactorily, to which the Logician replies, "Obviously, my dear sir, but now the problem is correctly posed." [4] Logic, by posing the question correctly, according to its own rules, can nullify any understanding of what is beyond its province. Now that the Logician has added his clarification, the rhinoceros may be psychical as well as physical.

In a remarkable episode in the first act, Jean and Bérenger are at one table discussing proper conduct. At another table on the opposite side of the stage, the Logician is explaining logic to an Old Gentleman. The two conversations, which overlap, have to be heard for the comic effectiveness to be fully realized. The Logician provides an example of a syllogism:

LOGICIAN: The cat has four paws. Isidore and Fricot both have four paws. Therefore Isidore and Fricot are cats.

OLD GENTLEMAN: My dog has got four paws.
LOGICIAN: Then it's a cat.

The Old Gentleman is impressed by the beauty of logic and The Logician is encouraged to supply further examples. "All cats die. Socrates is dead. Therefore Socrates is a cat." To which the Old Gentleman replies: "And he's got four paws. That's true. I've got a cat named Socrates." [5] While the Logician is proving at great pains the precision of the rigorously logical, Jean is providing a similar example of the correctness of moral precepts, and both in almost the same sentence at the same time pronounce equally illogical standards for understanding life. Theoretical abstractions imposed on events deny the uncertainty of experience. Meaning has departed from language and logical order proves the absurd. Only the trumpeting of another rhinoceros is able to interrupt their seriousness.

The scene shifts to the office where Bérenger works. Those who have not seen the rhinoceros provide equally ridiculous explanations according to their own particular political or philosophic predispositions. Botard, the union representative, a former school teacher and confirmed materialist, arrogant and self-important, interprets all events by incontrovertible Marxist principles, deciding the rhinoceros is an example of "collective psychosis. . . . Just like religion—the opiate of the people!" [6] Dudard, a well-mannered social climber, goes along with the majority opinion, anxious to do his duty. Daisy, the lovely secretary whom Bérenger wants to marry, is swept along by social pressures, unable to believe the evidence of her own eyes. Bérenger, lacking a fixed ideology and basically unpretentious, remains open to further proof and refuses to accept ardently imposed distortions.

Mrs. Boeuf enters to explain why her husband is late for work. He has not returned from a weekend visit to his family. A loud anguished trumpeting is heard outside and a powerful rhinoceros crashes into the building, destroying the staircase. The beast remains below, stomping, turning round and round, and uttering violent but tender groans. Mrs. Boeuf, recognizing her husband's voice, leaps from the window and lands on the rhinoceros's back, saying "Here I am, my sweet, I'm here now," [7] and off they go. People are turning into rhinoceroses.

Bérenger visits Jean, who gradually is metamorphosed into a horned beast: there is a change in the color of his skin, a huskiness in his voice, a lump in his forehead which grows larger and larger. As he changes physically, he also adjusts his morality to the new conditions. He had been a man without principles, preserving outward appearances. He refuses at first to admit that his physical nature is being transformed, then accepts it subconsciously, saying that if a man "changes into a rhinoceros on purpose or against his will, it's probably all for the better." Bérenger protests that men have moral standards and a "set of values, which it's taken centuries of human civilization to build up." Jean, who had defended propriety, can only say, "Are you under the impression that our way of life is superior? . . . I'm sick of moral standards! We need to go beyond moral standards!" [8] Jean has been easily defeated, now putting the law of nature and the rules of the jungle above the edicts of civilized society. At the end of the scene, now a full rhinoceros with a large horn on his head, he drops all pretense of outward civility. Trumpeting and snorting, he shouts to Bérenger, "I'll trample you, I'll trample you down!"

All the others relinquish their individuality, their values, and become rhinoceroses, including the Logician. Botard decides to join with the masses and the growing community spirit. Dudard says that all values are relative and that he will not desert his friends. Daisy and Bérenger are the only ones who have not succumbed. They stand alone on the balcony watching the swirling herds charge and snort below. He tells her that their love will keep them strong, that the world has gone mad, that in spite of a collapse of human values they can have children and regenerate the human race. She promises never to desert him, but the noise of the beasts grows more attractive to her. She feels lonely and lost, and lacks the courage to resist. Social pressure overwhelms her. She finds the appearance of the rhinoceroses pleasant: "They look happy. They're content to be what they are. . . . They were right to do what they did." She feels ashamed of love, which she condemns as a male weakness, for it lacks the energy and vitality of the snorting green monsters. Their clumsy movements now seem to her a graceful dance, their thick skins and green color lovely. "They are like gods," she exclaims, and dashes off to join the herd.[9]

Bérenger is now alone, the last human left on earth, experiencing the terrible loneliness of the individual in a dehumanized society. His final monologue is a desperate struggle to understand, to resist. He doubts his own ability to remain a human being in a society of rhinoceroses. Perhaps they are better looking, perhaps horns are more attractive. His value judgments change, his sense of beauty responds to the new criteria: "Oh I'd love to have a hard skin in that wonderful dull green color." He feels that he should join the others, but something deep within him prevents him from doing so, something that persists in remaining human in a non-human world, something within him that persists in holding on to man's dignity. He decides that he will fight: "I'm the last man left, and I'm staying that way until the end. I'm not capitulating!"[10]

Rhinoceros is the only play of Ionesco in which there is a positive declaration of hope, albeit a minimal one. Bérenger is not sure why he resists rhinoceritis, but he is a man free from ideologies and group slogans. His resistance arises from a deep natural element of man that seeks spiritual vitality and freedom of choice, and is unencumbered by preset notions. For this reason, Ionesco stated that his "resistance is genuine, profound."[11]

The origin of the play stems from an account by Denis de Rougemont of his experiences while waiting in the crowd for the arrival of Adolf Hitler. Although at first he felt removed and isolated from the emotional surge of those who surrounded him, as the Führer came nearer their hysteria mounted and he "felt the same raging madness in himself, struggling to possess him, a delirium that electrified him. He was on the point of falling under the spell when something rose from the depth of his being and resisted the rising storm." He felt terribly alone, "his hair stood on end . . . and he understood what is meant by Holy Terror."[12]

Ionesco was amazed at the popular success of the play and wondered whether audiences were aware of the "monstrous phenomenon of massification" to which they are constantly subjected. Perhaps, he argued, despite the attraction of stupefying conformism they are "in their heart of hearts all individualists, unique human beings." [13] In the Paris production, Jean-Louis Barrault presented the play as a fantastic fable, whereas in Germany it was offered as a tragedy. "Both interpretations," said Ionesco, "are valid exemplary productions of the play. *Rhinoceros* is both a farce and a tragedy." [14] Ionesco rejected the interpretation of the American production, which emphasized the comic elements. Jean as played by Zero Mostel was "a feeble rhinoceros" instead of a hard-set intolerant prig. Bérenger, whom Ionesco considered "an irresolute character, a reluctant hero, allergic to the epidemic of rhinoceritis," was turned into "a tough hard-headed individual, a kind of unruly revolutionary who knows quite well what he is doing." [15]

Bérenger remains pathetically but courageously alone in a world devoid of meaning, surrounded by loud trumpetings that proclaim absolute certainty. Jean-Paul Sartre attacked Ionesco for eschewing political involvement and declared that Bérenger resists "because he is Ionesco: he represents Ionesco, he says I resist, and there he remains in the midst of the rhinoceroses, the only one to defend man without our being very sure if it might not be better to be a rhinoceros. Nothing has been proved to the contrary." [16]

Ionesco needs no defense. The play speaks for itself. Sartre's position, advocacy of a particular political program, is precisely what Ionesco opposes. *Rhinoceros* is a magnificent theatrical demonstration of the ways in which the mind of man can be captured and enslaved by specific and transient doctrines, how easy and debasing it is to join the crowd, how difficult to stand alone. To Ionesco, the artist comes first, not the politician, the dreamer who believes in a metaphysical reality that asserts the unalterable dignity of man. "Ideology is not the source of art. A work of art is the source and the raw material of ideologies to come." [17]

II   *Pedestrian of the Air*—"There's nothing more
imprecise than precision."

In *Victims of Duty* Choubert is lifted into space by the living corpse and saved from the pursuing police. The idea of flying into outer space to defy death and escape the anxiety of this world is the central theme of *Pedestrian of the Air* (*Le Piéton de l'air*, 1963). On a lovely Sunday in Gloucestershire the people are out strolling, exchanging idle greetings, moving back and forth across the lovely landscape. A prying journalist interviews Bérenger, a French writer, who has retired to the English countryside because he is no longer able to write. There is no joy in being "able to say there was nothing to say." The avant-garde has been left behind by history, and it is "pointless to demystify what has been demystified already." [18]

Bérenger is of course Ionesco talking about himself or one facet of himself, now mocking his own work. He had used clichés to show the emptiness of bourgeois talk, now his own avant-garde phrases are revolutionary clichés. Life is a dreadful nightmare. Literature ought to be more cruel than reality. Imagination is the only means to leap beyond the emptiness of existence. Death is man's limitation. "I am paralyzed by the knowledge that I'm going to die. . . . I want to be cured of death." [19]

Bérenger, his wife, and his daughter Marthe join the other strollers, among whom are John Bull and The Bald Soprano, who was missing in Ionesco's first play and now makes a belated appearance. Only the very sensitive Marthe and Bérenger notice the Visitor from the Anti-World, a ghostly figure smoking an upside down pipe, who walks on air and then vanishes. Bérenger is overjoyed and explains that there are many universes, many anti-worlds, the negative of our universe, which we can understand if we examine our own thoughts, such as seeing "turrets of a castle reflected in the water, . . . or the sun's rays shining through a crystal prism." [20] Everything in our world, he explains, passes through the void on the other side and is upside down. Our only hope is that there everything will "be reconstructed and restored." [21] Intoxicated with happiness, Bérenger starts hopping about, jumping up and down, and then remains aloft, suspended in the air, walking above the ground. Trees and flowers appear and disappear from out of the void. A brilliant silver bridge arches the sky. Bérenger's will is on fire as he experiences weightlessness and a force bearing him upward. He jumps higher and higher and then vanishes across the silver bridge into outer space.

His wife Josephine remains behind helpless and abandoned and undergoes a painful self-analysis. A mock court of ghostly figures and death symbols acts out imagined fears. But Bérenger soon returns, exhausted and incoherent, recounting the horrors he has seen: "The men with the heads of geese"; "men licking the monkeys' behinds and drinking sows' piss"; guillotined men, marching along without their heads"; "giant grasshoppers and fallen angels." [22] The hope that lay on the other side of the world in other universes has vanished in a vision of colliding masses of ice and deserts of fire. There is no better world to which one can fly, only abysmal space and nothingness.

In the final scene, a Mardi Gras celebration of exploding fireworks against a red sky, Marthe provides the only remaining hope, that perhaps some day the "flames will die down, perhaps the ice will melt, perhaps the depths will rise." [23] Marthe has been closest to her father, sensitive to the world's despair, and her flickering note of optimism is the thin thread that permits survival.

III   *Exit the King*—"Tell me how you managed to accept death and die?"

In *Pedestrian of the Air* the entire play centers on the single fact of Bérenger's trip into outer space. In *Exit The King* (*Le Roi se meurt*, 1962) the single situation is that of a man awaiting death. Both plays run without intermission for an hour and a half and are extended parables, surrealist fantasies in high comic spirit revealing the underlying tragic theme of the senselessness of death.

Bérenger, the Everyman of the previous plays, is now King Bérenger I and is dying. In his dilapidated throne room he is surrounded by his two Queens and a Doctor who is also Surgeon, Executioner, Bacteriologist, and Astrologist. Queen Marguerite is practical and resigned, preparing the King to meet death gracefully, for like all men he too is mortal. She tells him in the opening scene, "You're going to die in an hour and a half, you're going to die at the end of the show." [24] The Doctor supplies the medical bulletins and adds that the chef has already turned off the gas as there will be no need for dinner that night. But Bérenger is King, with power over life and death, and refuses to accept the physical facts: "I'll die when I want to. I'm the King. I'm the one to decide." He is a combination of Alfred Jarry's grotesque Ubu Roi, who bumbles into catastrophe, and Albert Camus's Caligula, who, seeing that "men die and they are not happy," decides to restructure the universe, which as Emperor he believes he has the power to do. Bérenger, however, has little power left. The heating system doesn't work, the army has deserted, and the state too is dying, for the King's health is the health of the commonwealth. With memories of the past, Berenger makes a final bid for power. He orders "trees to sprout from the floor," "the roof to disappear," and "leaves to grow again," but nothing happens. He insists that kings should choose the moment of their death. The rigid structure of ordered society had set him in a position to determine the destiny of men. Now he wants to determine his own destiny. His only hope is his second wife, Queen Marie, young, beautiful and sensuous, who tells him that love can conquer death, that for those with passion for life there is no past or future, only the ever-enduring present. She is the symbol of Ionesco's nonlogical response, the world of incoherence, of refusal to accept scientific limitations. She is imagination, the senses feeding experience that has no boundaries and cannot be decreed by law. "Dive into an endless maze of wonder and surprise, then you too will have no end, and can exist forever. . . . Escape from definitions and you will breathe again!" [25]

The King cannot be consoled. To the "countless thousands" who have died before him he cries out, "Tell me how you managed to accept death and die?" [26] The King wants to know why each man must meet death as though it were a new experience. The Doctor supplies the latest facts of failing pulse, weakened limbs, and slowing heart; Queen Marie makes her final plea for love that destroys fear and lifts a man beyond himself into the universe that is one. The thoughtful, capable Queen Marguerite has the final say. She guides the King to his throne, helping him to move his arms and legs, now almost powerless. He takes his rightful seat, and in his final moments the walls, windows, and doors slowly disappear, as does the King himself, his throne bathed in a dimming green light and a rising mist.

Death, the unknown, the inevitable, has come, but not before Bérenger has had his moment of revenge. After crumpling and crawling on the floor, with the help of Queen Marguerite he finally stands erect, then sits on his throne staring straight ahead, no longer questioning but defiant, preserving the ultimate dignity of unconquerable resistance.

The single happening, as in *Amédée*, is overextended, but the subtle imagination, the precision and beauty of the language, the sharp mixture of utter banality with profound insight provide a classic grandeur of severe, sculptured proportions. Ionesco has completed the cycle from the absurdity of life in *The Bald Soprano* to the absurdity of death in *Exit the King*. Facing death as all men must is the test of life's values. To live a routine, mechanical existence and then to pass on with meek, unquestioning acceptance is hardly worthy of man who has mastered the forces of nature. Death for Ionesco remains a continuing scandal. His laughter is the triumph over death, at least for the moment.

CHAPTER 7

Hunger and Thirst and Massacre Games

> "I was so comfortable in my discomfort."
>
> *(Hunger and Thirst)*

IN February 1966 *Hunger and Thirst* (*La Soif et la faim*) opened at the Comédie-Française in Paris and precipitated the expected controversy that had now become usual for an Ionesco opening. Scandalized patrons hurled insults at the actors and walked out, condemning the play as another unnecessary portrayal of defeat and pessimism, a collection of surrealist trickery, a diluted repetition of absurdist clichés, hardly worthy of the man who aspired to be the next man of letters chosen for election to the French Academy.[1]

Ionesco had never pretended to be a messenger of hope. In *Hunger and Thirst* he had once more created a world of the imagination, a symbolic representation of the futile search for joy, a nightmarish adventure of the ordinary man in pursuit of love he cannot recognize, an ironic and perverse odyssey in a form more coherent and less bizarre than the earlier plays, and highly theatrical. Anticipating the Paris reception, Ionesco had arranged for the world premiere to take place the year before in Düsseldorf before a less belligerent audience of world diplomats, foreign correspondent, and the literary elite.

About his first play Ionesco had written: "the people in *The Bald Soprano* have no hunger, no conscious desires; they are bored stiff."[2] In *Hunger and Thirst* Jean, the central character, is conscious of his hunger but his search to appease it is undirected and fruitless, for like all men he seeks the absolute in a world that is relative, uncertain, and transient. The title of the play is a biblical reference. When asked whether he was a Christian, Ionesco replied, "I don't know if I'm a Christian or not, religious or not, a mystic or not; only that I have a Christian background. We all have hunger and thirst, many hungers and thirsts for earthly things, for water, for whiskey, for bread, for love, and for the absolute. Bread, wine, and meat for which Jean hungers are only substitutes for the deeper hunger and thirst for the absolute." [3]

The play is in three episodes, "The Flight," "The Rendezvous," and "The Black Masses of the Good Inn." For the American premiere which took place at the Berkshire Theatre Festival in July 1969, "The Rendezvous" was replaced by a completely rewritten second episode called "At the Foot of the Wall." For the American production, Ionesco supplied a summary of the play.

"Hunger and Thirst" is the story of Jean, a man who leaves his home—where he might discover a spiritual joy he fails to see within himself—to seek an improbable happiness, a key to the mysteries of life. He will not succeed in piercing the wall of knowledge: he finds only a world of anguish and distress—a place, the Inn, perhaps a reflection of our infernal world where fanatical and contradictory ideologies cancel each other out—sadness and emptiness. There will remain for Jean hope for the truth and happiness he has hidden from himself, a luminous virtue not totally lost and perhaps not discovered too late, love.[4]

I   *"The Flight"*

In a dark, dismal room Jean lives with his wife and child. Marie is happy, for she needs no more than the man she loves and the child she has borne to transform her drab surroundings into beauty. Jean is restless, complaining of the lack of light, the shabby furniture, the mildew and disintegration. He longs for sun and flowers and "boundless joy and ecstasy." [5] Marie represents everyday compromise, adjustment to necessity: she urges Jean to see with her eyes and create another reality with the power of love.

Aunt Adelaide enters out of the spectral recesses of the background and talks incessantly of her triumphs, her wealth, her adventures. With her Jean reverses his position and becomes the pragmatist, blasting her fantasies, bluntly reminding her that she is insane, poverty-stricken, a beggar, and dead. Adelaide denies his charges: "I move, I speak, I can talk. . . . I have a beautiful bosom." She opens her blouse, removes her brassiere, and shows her naked breasts. "Your wife can look too. Are hers as lovely as mine? . . . These are not the breasts of a ghost." [6] Marie, who had pleaded with her husband to abandon the disturbing rejection of fact, encourages Adelaide's fancies and urges her to come back another time for lunch. Adelaide, insistent upon proving she is alive, takes out a knife and slits her skull, then vanishes, her form remaining visible in the mirror until she disappears.

With Adelaide gone Jean resumes his longing for "memories I've never had" for mountain air where "death is not allowed." He had refused to permit Aunt Adelaide her dreams and self-created reality, had demanded that she face conventional truth as Marie had done with him, had uttered the platitudes of common sense adjustment; yet now he insists that he doesn't want to be like the others nor "get stuck in a rut." Marie replies that "all houses are tombs" and that he "cannot tear out the roots of love." As she talks, Jean appears and disappears. They engage in a game of hide-and-seek. Marie frantically tries to find him behind the sofa, under the tablecloth, in the drawers and cupboards. She dashes out in panic. Jean reappears momentarily, his face in pain as he tears from his heart a branch of briar rose and tiptoes out on his way to find "the sunlit park" where "you can see the ocean meet the sky." Marie returns, sees the branch of roses, and chants, "He really has torn out the flower of love, pulled it up by the roots." The rear wall opens and in its place rises a garden with green grass and trees in bloom. Marie closes the first episode saying, "He didn't know *that* was here! . . . If only he'd known! If he'd had a little patience, he wouldn't have gone, he wouldn't have left us behind!" [7]

The Lost Paradise is a repeated theme of Ionesco's work. Amédée, Choubert, the Old Man, Bérenger in earlier plays have had glimmering visions of a golden past, a time of happiness which contemporary anxieties no longer permit. In *Hunger and Thirst* the theme has been varied. The eternal sunlight, the blossoming gardens, the pure mountain air are no longer a forgotten past but a way of seeing. To control the chaos of experience, reason has imposed a learning process which dictates perception. To break from these prescribed dictates is painful but necessary. Marie sees the sunlight around her through the power of love, Adelaide finds happiness in the joy of her private fantasies, Jean moves actively in pursuit of a Paradise which he will never find, for he cannot recognize love when it surrounds him.

II *"The Rendezvous"*

In the original version Jean is on a mountaintop near a museum, where he awaits the ideal woman, who never appears. He has been wandering for years and is now talking to the two uniformed keepers of the museum. He says, "I'm a different person, yet I'm still the same one. I'd got too involved in things." A parenthetical jibe is leveled at existentialism. Jean is not the sum of his actions. He can "throw them off" and find that he still is in one piece. When the woman of his dreams, past or future, the incarnation of joy he is seeking, does not keep the rendezvous, Jean is in despair. "I've no other refuge but you. There's nowhere I can live now. . . . I was so comfortable in my discomfort! . . . I wanted to escape old age, keep out of a rut. It's life I'm looking for! Joy I'm after! I've longed for fulfillment and all I find is torment." [8] The inchoate cry, the unrelieved search, are expressed in Jean's platitudes, which are answered by a contradictory set of platitudes and incongruities by the listening keepers, the anonymous commentators on human frailty.

> 2ND KEEPER: Who claimed we should be free
>   from the ties that bind us?
> 1ST KEEPER: Who said nobody and nothing could
>   ever belong to us?
> 2ND KEEPER: What a breach between heart
>   and head!
> 1ST KEEPER: What a contradiction!
> 2ND KEEPER: He doesn't believe what he thinks
>   or think what he believes. [9]

Jean is disturbed, disappointed, and persistently irrational: "I know there's no reason for living. . . . I found a *non*-reason . . . I clung to it and my hands got bruised." The woman whose name he does not know, who represents memories and secret wishes that may never have existed, is for him "absolute necessity." He goes off to conquer the world, calling to the ideal woman who has never appeared, who may by chance appear somewhere else, who is his private and complete passion, "so dazzling, so gentle, intense and passionate and reassuring," [10] the one to lighten the darkness of his pilgrimage. The keepers go off to eat to appease physical hunger and thirst, enjoying the smell of soup and the taste of wine.

The episode is characteristic of the many waiting scenes in the theatre of the absurd, stemming from Beckett's *Waiting for Godot*. Chekhov had provided plays in which life changes while people sit around, talking, eating, and hurting one another unknowingly out of the best intentions; but his characters are recognizable human beings, while Beckett's waiting figures are embodiments of abstract concepts, representations of despair and futility, who pass the time by engaging in idle conversation and performing simple everyday physical acts. Jean, unlike Vladimir and Estragon in *Waiting for Godot*, moves off at the end of the scene, but his continual movement is another aspect of endless waiting. Behind the total emptiness and unfulfilled dreams lies a vague, incoherently articulated hope.

This episode was omitted from the American production and a completely different one, "The Foot of the Wall," was substituted. Jean arrives at a huge wall, around which he cannot go and through which the door is barred. On the wall are hieroglyphs, ideograms, and primitive reliefs—adornments on the Wall of Knowledge. Tourists pass by, pausing to love, to laugh, and to picnic, as guides point out the attractions of the place. Two silly-voiced, mini-skirted girls, identical twins, appear with a young man who is engaged to one of them. The other, we never know precisely which, commits suicide in anger and frustration. The young man refuses to marry the remaining twin. A rabbi stops by with a band of bearded children, discusses philosophy with Jean, then as a logical consequence of his political views, leads the children to a precipice and sends them crashing to their death. He returns as a magician and opens the wall for Jean to enter.

Either version, "The Wall" or "The Rendezvous," is dramatically unsatisfactory and adds little to the overall impact. Ionesco removed the central section and replaced it with another as though he were dealing with pieces of a Chinese puzzle. He could just as well have included all four episodes in the final version, since plot development is of little consequence and the tight realistic form is discarded. The main function of the second act is to serve as a prelude for the final magnificent episode.

III   "*The Black Masses of the Good Inn*"

Jean finds himself in the refectory of a monastery. Brother Tarabas, a hooded monk, offers food and drink then introduces the Brother Superior, an abnormally tall figure in white robes. After his feet are washed, Jean is brought endless quantities of food and drink. He is amazed by his hunger and thirst. "I eat and drink, eat and drink. And still I'm thirsty, still hungry." He claims that he had ignored hunger, for "I was so engrossed in my adventures, in the beauty and the marvels of the countries I went through." [11] Jean sounds like a Cook's travel guide. A procession of monks brings in food and drink, moving in and out of the surrounding darkness. Jean is asked to tell the story of his travels, to reveal the marvels he has seen that had so absorbed him that he had neglected bodily needs. He can utter only dull phrases, trite repetitions of catalog description of places. Tarabas warns that incomplete news only increases their hunger and thirst, but Jean grows increasingly inarticulate. He has found no meaning, no insight to communicate. He has been the eternal pilgrim but not the poet in quest of the unknowable and the transcendent. He has sought beauty without being able to recognize it; he has longed for joy which he cannot experience. He is the insensitive commonplace man with the irresistible urge of an errant knight but the soul of a bourgeois pedestrian of the air. His description of the marvels he has seen is a series of babbling phrases.

Jean offers to pay his bill, but the Brother Superior insists that he first witness a play of "education and re-education." Two cages appear. Inside one is Brechtoll, who has no faith, and inside the other is Tripp, who does believe in God. The two are shoddy, unkempt prisoners who have evidently suffered for a long time. With Brother Tarabas as Inquisitor they undergo alternately and simultaneously their final interrogation. Food is held out to them if they will deny their beliefs. Both refuse, being men of principle and high ideals. On opposite sides of the stage, circling the separate cages, are the supporters of each prisoner. The monks on Brechtoll's side are dressed in red and flooded in red light, for the prisoner is an obvious follower of Bertolt Brecht. Those who applaud Tripp's position are in black gowns and white light. Each group responds with choral chant and mimetic rhythms when it approves a statement of its favorite. Jean is invited to take the central chair, and posed like a judge above the action he watches the performance. The scene is a ghoulish nightmare of hooded figures, relentless interrogation, and two wildly performing captives, forced to undergo the ritual of temptation. Unable to endure the physical torture and the razor edge of Tarabas's intellectual probing, Brechtoll and Tripp capitulate in a simultaneous staccato chorus, reversing their convictions. Brechtoll insists there is a God and Tripp denies His existence. As a reward, both are then given food. After eating they approach Tarabas and Jean, remove their costumes, and turn out to be actors who have performed a role, clowns in a carefully rehearsed program.

In this long and brilliant play within a play, Ionesco once again is lashing out at both commitment and conformity. Tripp is the average man, the upholder of tradition. Brechtoll is rebellion, opposition, the defender of a new moral order. Neither has the courage of his convictions. Niether can face death or starvation with the inner strength that certainty affords. Both fail under pressure, for they represent ludicrous surface postures which are not able to compete with the intensity of the primitive animal need to satisfy hunger and thirst.

Jean's sudden and inexhaustible hunger comes from the "hollow feeling inside . . . this gaping void I've never been able to fill." The theme of the Lost Paradise, the nostalgic past, recurs as Jean asks, "Why were there no more luminous days, why this gloom? . . . Was I or was I not meant to roam those twilit autumn roads in search of light?" [12] Jean again wants to pay his bill, and be given permission to go on his way, but the hooded monks are not ordinary innkeepers. The Brother Accountant figures that the amount Jean owes can be paid by service that will take all his remaining days. Jean cannot leave. He is compelled to discharge his debt by serving food to the monks. He rushes back and forth in increasing tempo, bringing the plates to the hooded Brothers seated at a long table. The Brothers take up a chant recounting the number of days Jean will have to serve. A picture of Marie and her now grown-up daughter appear in the "luminous garden" in the background, offering Jean love which he could not see. Marie calls out, "We'll wait! we'll wait! No matter how long, I'll wait for you," [13] in a choral counterpoint to the chanting of the monks.

The thirst for the absolute crashes against the absolute of thirst. Ideals are helpless in the face of primitive needs for survival. All commitment vanishes before the necessity to eat and drink. Jean is left with a futile dream performing menial service in an isolated Inn, surrounded by the gloom of skepticism and the mystery of the unknown, in a continuing ritual of the Black Mass.

IV   *Massacre Games*

At the time Ionesco was delivering his speech of acceptance in the French Academy, his new play *Massacre Games* (*Jeux de massacre*, 1970) was being presented at the Théâtre Montparnasse-Gaston-Baty. The dull traditional speech of a newly named Immortal was in sharp contrast to the same Immortal's comments in another bizarre parable on the inevitability of death. In *Exit the King* Bérenger dies after a feeble effort to determine the meaning of death. *Massacre Games*, the new play, has no central characters. In a nameless town in the throes of a mysterious plague every inhabitant goes to his death without the chance to raise questions.

The people parade back and forth in small groups in a series of vignettes. Actors can play several roles or can perform in masks, for they are nameless and interchangeable marionettes in the face of a common destiny. The old, the young, the merchants, the staid, the abnormal utter inconsequential bits of disconnected thoughts, refer to the plague and the way in which it will not affect them, and are suddenly stricken. In every scene the entire group onstage falls over and dies. An invisible monk moves in the background as the ever-present symbol of the dread Scourge.

Death strikes everywhere and everyone as Ionesco repeats his theme of the futility of life if man is not immortal. Jealousy, commitment, crime, even love are trivial banalities in the face of ubiquitous, uncertain, and unreasonable death. Camus had handled the same theme more effectively in *The Plague,* to which Ionesco is indebted, as he is even more so to Daniel Defoe's *Journal of the Plague Year.*

Massacre Games does not rank among Ionesco's more important plays and the premiere was not offered at a major Paris theatre. It is too repetitious, too deeply pessimistic, bordering on total nihilism. Mass death begins and ends the work, which is perhaps its weakness, for as one Paris critic remarked, "The play is not cruel enough." Mass killings eliminate personal empathy and the continued presence of death, particularly when it strikes suddenly and without pain, renders one impervious to whatever anguish may hide behind its impersonal destruction. In modern war, entire villages may be reduced to ashes and arouse less public concern than the saving of a single life with a heart transplant. *Exit the King,* about the death of one man, is more effective. *Massacre Games* is a ballet of death—cold, precise, and mechanical, Ionesco's definitive comment on the irrationality of death. A director's skill and technical inventiveness can keep the play from being too static, but the single conceit does not lend itself to too many variations.

Only brief mention can be made of *Macbett* presented at the Théâtre Rive-Gauche in February 1972 as this book was going to press. Ionesco at the age of sixty had taken Shakespeare's *Macbeth* and transformed it into a grotesque nightmare replete with a satanic dance, a crushed rebellion, mass slayings, confused identity and the repeated theme of liberators becoming tyrants. Malcolm, son of the murdered King, replaces Macduff as the slayer of Macbett and vows that he will inaugurate a more fearful reign of terror. The play, like *Massacre Games,* lacks the power and poetry of *Hunger and Thirst* and gives expression once more to Ionesco's deep pessimism in a world where Nothingness surrounds man in the contemporary breakdown of established order.

CHAPTER 8

The Paradox of the Illogical

"Dreams are . . . more substantial."

THE immortality that King Bérenger sought, Ionesco achieved by being elected to the French Academy, the illustrious body of Forty Immortals; but those who are chosen seek the honor by formal application and personal solicitation. Many of the best known writers of France have spurned membership, among them Molière, Pascal, Balzac, Camus, and Sartre. Why did Ionesco, leader of the avant-garde, relentless opponent of tradition, seek to be among the august upholders of tradition? The answer probably lies in the constant paradox that pursues Ionesco's work and the man himself. When Jean Cocteau, *enfant terrible* of French letters, was asked why he had sought election to the Academy, he replied that since so many great writers were not members, the true rebel could best serve by infiltrating their ranks. The reason for Ionesco's decision more likely lies in his morbid fear of death, a fear that haunts every page of the *Journal en miettes* and recurs in almost every play. Recognition of his place in literature offered material evidence of possible immortality. But his art can stand on its own merits and the Academy represents all that Ionesco had rejected in form, ideas, content, and spirit. He had earlier chosen to be Transcendent Satrap of the invisible College of 'Pataphysicians, for which he occasionally issued a white paper consisting mainly of interviews with himself. Membership in these two Academies symbolizes the enduring contradiction between the separate and divided worlds of fact and fancy.

The persistent themes of Ionesco's work reflect contemporary dislocation. Man's condition is absurd, for it has been devitalized by the cold confines of logic. Experience, imagination, feeling,

89

and dreams, the substance of life, have been ignored. "Logic is the surface of consciousness, dreams are much more profound consciousness, more substantial." [1] Freedom of the spirit is not an escape into the unreal but "daring and inventive . . . and invention is not abdication." [2] The free play of the senses and the spirit roams beyond the limits of reason. The first effort to achieve freedom lies in mocking Cartesian order, which has set boundaries that minimize the vitality of native intution. The essentially human is extrasocial, beyond economic and political alignments and commitment to temporary partisan causes. So long as man is mortal he will be enslaved by scientific limitations of time and space. To express these themes Ionesco employs a technique in opposition to established Aristotelian categories. In his plays space and time are elastic. Language disintegrates, contradictions persist, psychology is absent, objects assume a separate vitality of their own, normal situations are exaggerated, and conventional attitudes are distorted, reduced to absurdity in a series of surrealist images.

Ionesco's art, however, generates its own paradox. Feelings, passions, and dreams are not communicable. They are experiences that are private, intense, and boundless, and once communicated they are lost. To express the irrational world the imposition of form is necessary, for art is the means of ordering the chaos of emotions. But the order imposed is a new logic, a new set of strictures and limitations. The substitution of a new logic outside of Cartesian logic implies confinement in Ionesco's own didacticism.

The problem is unsolvable and self-contradictory, and Ionesco is as fully fond of contradictions as the porter in *Macbeth* who says, "Here's an equivocator, that could swear in both the scales against either scale." Strindberg, to give dramatic expression to the subconscious, created a new form in his dream plays, retaining as little of the old form as possible, but enough of it, words for example, to make it comprehensible. No revolution can be completely new. It must drag along enough of the old to provide comprehensibility and continuity. Ionesco likewise creates a distinct and separate form out of necessity, a form which startled and shocked in *The Bald Soprano* but became acceptable and familiar in *Hunger and Thirst*. Audiences adjust quickly unless the form is constantly replenished by endless inventiveness. The avant-garde in time becomes part of the Establishment and a new avant-garde comes into being as the artist rejects the sterility of imposed paradigms. The outlandishly bizarre College of 'Pataphysicians became a tolerated phenomenon of the current scene that could easily, with some political conniving, be accepted as a branch of the Sorbonne.

Ionesco rose out of Strindberg, Kafka, and de Chirico. He is generally recognized as the master of the theatre of the irrational, to whom absurdist playwrights ever since have been indebted, including Harold Pinter, Joe Orton, N. F. Simpson, Edward Albee, Arthur Kopit, Sam Shepard, and a host of others. Ionesco's plays, removed from psychology and introspection, are a return to ritual and ceremony, to symbol and fantasy, a theatre of experience which is at a refreshing remove from the dull, living-room domestic drama. The breakdown of realism and logic has affected every aspect of stage life and has been the basis of a revolution in theatrical expression.

Ionesco does not offer a profound philosophic insight, but his tragic clowning has provided, in the true function of the playwright, an awareness of a mad, illogical world that may be plunging headlong into total destruction. In the final analysis Ionesco's images are designed to reassert faith in man. When the astronauts landed on the moon, this deeply pessimistic herald of the death of God and science wrote with compassion, "We know how the earth is, we have seen it from space, we know it is the most beautiful of the stars and we pronounce the name of God in space." [3]

Notes and References

Special Note: Quotations from Ionesco's plays are for the most part from the editions cited. Where liberties have been taken with the translations or where I have supplied my own, no page reference is indicated.

Chapter One

1. Eugène Ionesco, "The World of Ionesco," *Tulane Drama Review*, III (October 1958), p. 47.
2. *Ibid.*
3. *Ibid.*
4. *Ibid.*
5. William Barrett, *Irrational Man* (New York, 1962), p. 35.
6. Louis Mumford, "The Megamachine," *The New Yorker Magazine*, 10 October 1970.
7. Barrett, p. 64.
8. For further information on the College of 'Pataphysics see Tom Bishop, "Ionesco on Olympus," *Saturday Review*, 16 May 1970; John Wilcock, "The College of 'Pataphysics," *Village Voice*, 18 November 1965; Richard N. Coe, *Ionesco* (London and Edinburgh, 1961), Chapter I.
9. Antonin Artaud, *The Theatre and Its Double*, trans. Mary C. Richards (New York, 1958), p. 79.
10. *Ibid.*, p. 9.

Chapter Two

1. Bishop, "Ionesco on Olympus."
2. Eugène Ionesco, *Notes and Counter Notes*, trans. Donald Watson (New York, 1964), p. 16.
3. *Premières Mondiales*, Institut International du Théâtre, Paris, October, 1959.
4. *Notes and Counter Notes*, p. 186.
5. *Ibid.*, p. 186.

6. "The World of Ionesco" p. 47.

7. Claude Bonnefoy, *Entretiens avec Eugène Ionesco* (Paris, 1966), p. 126.

8. *Notes and Counter Notes*, p. 235.

9. *Ibid.*, p. 89.

10. *Ibid.*, p. 91.

11. *Ibid.*, p. 127.

12. *Ibid.*, p. 29.

13. *Ibid.*, p. 79.

14. *Ibid.*, p. 195.

15. *Ibid.*, p. 9.

16. Eugène Ionesco, *Four Plays* (*The Bald Soprano; The Lesson; Jack or The Submission; The Chairs*), trans. Donald M. Allen (New York, 1958), pp. 91–92.

17. *Notes and Counter Notes*, p. 54.

18. *Ibid.*, p. 63.

19. Bonnefoy, p. 80.

20. *Ibid.*, p. 80.

21. *Notes and Counter Notes*, p. 15.

22. *Ibid.*, p. 25.

23. Bonnefoy, p. 68.

24. *Notes and Counter Notes*, p. 81.

25. *The Bald Soprano*, p. 34.

26. *Ibid.*, p. 12.

27. Bonnefoy, p. 84.

28. Eugène Ionesco, *The Killer and Other Plays* (*Improvisation or The Shepherd's Chameleon; Maid to Marry*), trans. Donald Watson (New York, 1960), p. 118.

29. Bonnefoy, p. 110.

30. *Ibid.*, p. 71.

31. *Ibid.*, p. 93.

32. *Notes and Counter Notes*, p. 11.

33. *The Bald Soprano*, p. 38.

34. *The Chairs*, p. 148.

35. Eugène Ionesco, *Three Plays* (*Amédée or How to Get Rid of It; The New Tenant; Victims of Duty*), trans. Donald Watson (New York, 1958), p. 158.

36. *Notes and Counter Notes*, p. 29.

37. Bonnefoy, pp. 125–126.

38. Bonnefoy, p. 13.

39. *Victims of Duty*, pp. 117–118.

40. *Victims of Duty*, p. 130.

41. Eugène Ionesco, *Journal en miettes* (Paris, 1967), p. 171.
42. Bonnefoy, p. 125.

Chapter Three

1. *Notes and Counter Notes*, p. 28.
2. *Ibid.*, p. 179.
3. *The Bald Soprano*, p. 8.
4. *Ibid.*, p. 12.
5. *Notes and Counter Notes*, p. 197.
6. *The Bald Soprano*, p. 18.
7. *Notes and Counter Notes*, p. 176.
8. *The Bald Soprano*, pp. 36–37.
9. "The World of Eugène Ionesco," p. 46.
10. *Ibid.*
11. *Ibid.*
12. *Notes and Counter Notes*, p. 175.
13. *Ibid.*, p. 180.
14. *The Lesson*, p. 76.
15. *Ibid.*, p. 78.
16. *Ibid.*, p. 55.
17. *Ibid.*, p. 69.
18. *Notes and Counter Notes*, p. 182.
19. *The Chairs*, p. 159.
20. "The World of Ionesco," p. 46.
21. *Notes and Counter Notes*, pp. 188–189.
22. Simone Benmussa, *Ionesco* (Paris, 1966), p. 131.

Chapter Four

1. *Notes and Counter Notes*, pp. 194–195.
2. "The World of Ionesco," p. 47.
3. *Jack or The Submission*, p. 80.
4. *Ibid.*, p. 81.
5. *Ibid.*, p. 84.
6. *Ibid.*, pp. 91–92.
7. *Ibid.*, p. 104.
8. *Ibid.*, p. 108.
9. *Ibid.*, pp. 109–110.
10. *The New Tenant*, p. 98.
11. *Notes and Counter Notes*, p. 84.
12. *Ibid.*, p. 84.
13. *Victims of Duty*, pp. 117–118.
14. *Ibid.*, p. 118.

15. *Ibid.*, p. 120.
16. *Ibid.*, p. 128.
17. *Ibid.*, p. 130.
18. *Ibid.*, p. 138.
19. *Ibid.*, p. 144.
20. *Ibid.*, p. 158.
21. *Ibid.*, p. 159.
22. *Improvisations*, p. 118.
23. *Ibid.*, pp. 149–150.

Chapter Five

1. Bonnefoy, pp. 96–97.
2. *Notes and Counter Notes*, p. 196.
3. *Amédée*, p. 39.
4. *Ibid.*, p. 47.
5. *Ibid.*, p. 75.
6. *Ibid.*, p. 77.
7. *Notes and Counter Notes*, p. 196.
8. *The Killer*, p. 12.
9. *Ibid.*, p. 19. The translation has been changed to emphasize the conflict between the inner self and the outer self.
10. *Ibid.*, p. 26.
11. *Ibid.*, p. 83.
12. *Ibid.*, p. 108.
13. *Ibid.*, p. 109.

Chapter Six

1. *Notes and Counter Notes*, p. 211.
2. Interview in *New York Times*, January 31, 1960.
3. *Notes and Counter Notes*, p. 209.
4. Eugène Ionesco, *Rhinoceros and Other Plays* (*Rhinoceros; The Leader; The Future Is in Eggs or It Takes All Sorts to Make a World*), trans. Derek Prouse (London, 1960), pp. 36–37.
5. *Rhinoceros*, pp. 18–19.
6. *Ibid.*, p. 45.
7. *Ibid.*, p. 52.
8. *Ibid.*. p. 67.
9. *Ibid.*, pp. 103–104.
10. *Ibid.*, p. 107.
11. *Notes and Counter Notes*, p. 199.
12. *Ibid.*, p. 198.
13. *Ibid.*, p. 211.

14. *Ibid.,* p. 207.

15. *Ibid.,* p. 207.

16. Jean-Paul Sartre, "Beyond Bourgeois Theatre," *Tulane Drama Review,* V (March, 1961), 6.

17. *Notes and Counter Notes,* p. 93.

18. Eugène Ionesco, *A Stroll in the Air and Frenzy for Two, or More,* trans. Donald Watson (New York, 1965), pp. 21–22. *A Stroll in the Air* has also been translated as *Pedestrian of the Air,* the title used in this chapter.

19. *Pedestrian of the Air,* p. 23.

20. *Ibid.,* p. 52.

21. *Ibid.,* p. 54.

22. *Ibid.,* pp. 112–113.

23. *Pedestrian of the Air,* p. 117.

24. Eugène Ionesco, *Plays, Volume V (Exit the King; Foursome; The Motor Show),* trans. Donald Watson (London, 1963), p. 20.

25. *Exit the King,* p. 50.

26. *Exit the King,* p. 53.

Chapter Seven

1. *Nouvel Observatoire* (Paris), September 21, 1970, pp. 44–45.

2. "The World of Ionesco," p. 46.

3. Benmussa, p. 8.

4. Berkshire Theatre Festival, Summer 1969, Program Notes.

5. Eugène Ionesco, *Hunger and Thirst and Other Plays (Hunger and Thirst; The Picture; Anger; Salutations),* trans. Donald Watson (New York, 1968), p. 14.

6. *Hunger and Thirst,* p. 23.

7. *Ibid.,* pp. 35–36.

8. *Ibid.,* p. 46.

9. *Ibid.,* pp. 47–48.

10. *Ibid.,* pp. 50–51.

11. *Ibid.,* p. 56.

12. *Ibid.,* p. 98.

13. *Ibid.,* p. 106.

Chapter Eight

1. Bonnefoy, p. 90.

2. *Notes and Counter Notes,* p. 82.

3. *New York Times,* July 21, 1969.

Selected Bibliography

PRIMARY SOURCES

Four Plays, trans. Donald M. Allen. New York: Grove Press, 1958. (Includes *The Bald Soprano; The Lesson; Jack or The Submission; The Chairs.*)

Three Plays, trans. Donald Watson. New York: Grove Press, 1958. (Includes *Amédée or How to Get Rid of It; The New Tenant; Victims of Duty.*)

The Killer and Other Plays, trans. Donald Watson. New York: Grove Press, 1960. (Includes *The Killer; Improvisation or The Shepherd's Chameleon; Maid to Marry.*)

Rhinoceros and Other Plays, trans. Derek Prouse. London: John Calder, 1960. (Includes *Rhinoceros; The Leader; The Future Is in Eggs or It Takes All Sorts to Make a World.*)

Plays, Volume V, trans. Donald Watson. London: John Calder, 1963. (Includes *Exit the King; Foursome; The Motor Show.*)

Notes and Counter Notes, trans. Donald Watson. New York: Grove Press, 1964.

Plays, Volume VI, trans. Donald Watson. New York: Grove Press, 1965. (Includes *A Stroll in the Air* [*Pedestrian of the Air*]; *Frenzy for Two or More.*)

Journal en miettes, Paris: Mercure de France, 1967.

Hunger and Thirst and Other Plays, trans. Donald Watson. New York: Grove Press, 1968. (Includes *Hunger and Thirst; The Picture; Anger; Salutations.*)

Jeux de massacre. Paris: Editions Gallimard, 1970.

Présent passé Passé présent. Paris: Mercure de France, 1968.

"The World of Ionesco," *International Theatre Annual*, No. 2, ed. Harold Hobson. London: John Calder, 1957. Reprinted in *Tulane Drama Review*, III (October 1958), 46–48.

SECONDARY SOURCES

BENMUSSA, SIMONE. "Les Ensevelis dans le théâtre d'Eugène Ionesco," *Cahiers de la Compagnie Madeleine Renaud-Jean-Louis Barrault,* 22, 23 (May 1958), pp. 197–207.

BENMUSSA, SIMONE. *Ionesco.* Théâtre de tous les temps. Paris: Editions Seghers, 1966. Excellent analysis of the plays, including *Hunger and Thirst,* with critical articles by Ionesco and an extensive bibliography.

BONNEFOY, CLAUDE. *Entretiens avec Eugène Ionesco.* Paris: Editions Pierre Belfond, 1966. Ionesco discusses his work, his critics, and his plans.

COE, RICHARD N. *Ionesco.* Writers and Critics series. London and Edinburgh: Oliver and Boyd Ltd., 1961. The basic themes of Ionesco's work carefully outlined but unfortunately not in chronological order.

DRIVER, TOM F. *Romantic Quest and Modern Query.* New York: Delacorte Press, 1970. Chapter 14, pp. 346–390. Contains a sobering chapter on Ionesco's place in contemporary theatre.

ESSLIN, MARTIN. *The Theatre of the Absurd.* Anchor Books ed. Garden City: Doubleday, 1961. pp. 79–140. A keen critical insight by one of the first critics to give Ionesco full recognition.

GOUHIER, HENRI. "Eugène Ionesco," *La table ronde,* No. 137 (May 1959), pp. 176–180.

GROSSVOGEL, DAVID I. *The Blasphemers: The Theater of Brecht, Ionesco, Beckett, Genet.* Ithaca: Cornell University Press, 1962. Good for general reference.

GUICHARNAUD, JACQUES. *Modern French Theatre from Giraudoux to Beckett.* New Haven: Yale University Press, 1961. Brief treatment of Ionesco's "world out of control."

JACOBSEN, JOSEPHINE and WILLIAM R. MUELLER. *Ionesco and Genet: Playwrights of Silence.* New York: Hill and Wang, 1968. Extremely intelligent analysis of the plays but more concerned with literary rather than dramatic aspects of Ionesco's work. A basic reference book.

LEWIS, ALLAN. *The Contemporary Theatre.* Rev. ed., New York: Crown Publishers, Inc., 1971. Chapter on Ionesco analyzes the most recent plays and gives due credit to Ionesco as a major influence in the revolt of the irrational.

PRONKO, LEONARD CABELL. *Avant-Garde: The Experimental Theater in France.* Berkeley and Los Angeles: University of California Press, 1966. A general summary.

ROBBE-GRILLET, ALAIN. "Eugène Ionesco," *Critique*, No. 73. (June 1953), pp. 564–565.

SAROYAN, WILLIAM. "Ionesco" *Theatre Arts* (New York), (July 1958).

TYNAN, KENNETH, ORSON WELLES, PHILIP TOYNBEE, EUGÈNE IONESCO, and others. Articles first printed in the *Observer*, 22 and 29 June, 6 and 13 July, 1958. Reprinted under title "Ionesco à l'heure anglaise" in *Théâtre populaire*, No. 34 (1959), pp. 129–141. Reprinted in Eugène Ionesco's *Notes and Counter Notes*.

WATSON, DONALD. "The Plays of Eugène Ionesco," *Tulane Drama Review*, III (October 1958), 48–53. A brief, stimulating article by Ionesco's English translator.

WELLWARTH, GEORGE E. *The Theater of Protest and Paradox.* New York: New York University Press, 1964. An excellent secondary source that summarizes much of the available material.

APPENDIX A

Politics and Art: The London Controversy

IN 1955, the Royal Court Theatre of London revived two early one-act plays of Ionesco. The occasion marked the return of Joan Plowright to the scene of her earlier triumphs after a successful appearance in the United States and offered her the opportunity to display her versatility as an actress, playing the ninety-year-old hag in *The Chairs* and the doltish teenage doctoral student in *The Lesson*. It proved a triumph for the redoubtable patron saint of the English experimental theatre but even a greater triumph for Ionesco who was enthusiastically hailed as the uncontested leader of the avant garde. Kenneth Tynan, well known drama critic who had led the fight for Ionesco five years earlier, launched an attack on what he felt was the dangerous acceptance of a new messiah. The basis of his argument was that total rejection of realism and the cultish acceptance of anti-theatre could lead to a rejection of humanistic values and an increase of frustration and despair. If man was to survive there must be an alternative to mechanical robots disintegrating in the accumulation of things and the absence of communication. Realism, though badly battered as an art form, at least preserved faith in man and encouraged political action.

Ionesco defended his oft repeated thesis that he had no desire to save humanity which was more properly the concern of statesmen and economists, that his world of the imagination was beyond immediate political issues, that communication of people consists in their common anguish and isolation and that realism was obsolete since it is the art form of the cult of Reason. The debate by Tynan and Ionesco was joined by others in what is now known

as the London Controversy. Ionesco survived the heated arguments and went on to write his best plays, including *Rhinoceros,*
his most explicit anti-fascist statement. Kenneth Tynan retired
as critic, joined the Royal Shakespeare Company as literary ad-
visor, and then produced the financially successful pornographic
review *Oh! Calcutta!* The controversy, however, raised the important question of the validity of realism as an art form and the
more volatile issue of the writer's obligation to society which has
been the subject of continued and often acrimonious debate ever
since. This problem is dealt with briefly in Chapter Two. It is here
presented in greater detail since it does not properly belong in
a section devoted to the development of style. Extracts from Kenneth Tynan's article, Ionesco's reply, and comments by Philip
Toynbee and Orson Welles are appended.

The relationship of art to society and the corollary question of
the extent to which a writer should be involved in political action
is an extremely complex question. Unfortunately, most partici-
pants in the debate are so involved in particular personal projects
that they ignore the fact that the answers depend largely on the
historical moment. In times of comparative social tranquility, the
question is largely academic and writers pursue their lives guided
by individual conscience and political conviction. A lone Arnold
Wesker uses the theatre as a weapon in the class struggle seeking
to rescue the proletariat somewhat belatedly while surrounded
by less politically conscious and far more imaginative playwrights like Joe Orton or N. F. Simpson. Wesker's trenchant call
for a socially conscious attack on the Establishment fell on in-
dulgent but apathetic ears and he soon retreated from his original
position.

In times of political crisis the writer like most citizens is compelled to take sides. Germany during the days of the Weimar
Republic became the battleground for the future. The defeat of
the Kaiser's armies left a nation in disequilibrium, fertile ground
for the fight between Communism and National Socialism for
eventual control. In the theatre, within a few years of each other,

Friedrich Wolf presented *The Sailors of Cattaro,* a lyric apostrophe to the mutinous sailors of the Austrian navy and their martyrdom for freedom, whereas Hanns Johst dedicated his play *Schlageter* to Adolph Hitler, a play in which occur the lines attributed to Göring, "When I hear *Kultur* I loosen the safety catch on my revolver." Writers could not afford the luxury of remaining on the sidelines. The fate of Western civilization was in the balance.

Similarly in the United States during the days of the Great Depression when writers for the first time were organized into trade unions, the cry "Writer, take your stand!" was heard on all sides. Albert Maltz, a left-wing writer, was severely criticized by the *New Masses,* organ of the left wing movement, for advocating that a writer make his major contribution by writing rather than by standing on picket lines. When Luigi Pirandello arrived in the United States for lecture appearances, Clifford Odets led a contingent of American writers to confront the Nobel Prize winner and demand that he speak out against Mussolini. Pirandello, whose work, like Ionesco's, lies in the realm of fantasy and the non-political, refused to commit himself. He was satisfied that Mussolini had given him a theatre in which he could present his plays. Arthur Miller, a stalwart defender of social reform insisted that the writer must share responsibility for the world he himself has helped to make and that he should not resist from placing blame. The implication is that in the choice of moralities there is a correct one. In "After the Fall" a later play, Arthur Miller retreated from moral certainty and placed blame on an eternal constant human nature from Adam to Arthur which is capable of violence and destruction.

Intense partisanship generated in the heat of political battle has not helped in resolving a difficult problem. All artists "take a stand" for if the function of art is to establish order out of chaos the artist imposes on his raw material the essential ingredients of selection, emphasis, exaggeration and distortion which imply a point of view. That point of view is either an implicit defense of existing institutions or a call for radical change. Even the most innocuous Broadway commercial comedy portrays established mores in danger but happily restored. The question boils down not to one of commitment in general but of specific political commitment at a particular moment in history and varies with a writer's basic philosophy which too may alter with events. Zola's resounding "J'accuse!" in the Dreyfus Affair stemmed from long dedication to exposing moral corruption of a materialist oriented industrial society and was a plausible extension of his own creed. Jean-Paul Sartre, a member of the Resistance, close to the Communist Party at varying times in his career issued the call for "*engagement,*" claiming with Camus that to deserve the right to influence men who struggle it is necessary to take part in that struggle, or in the words of *Les Mains sales* to be willing to get one's hands dirty, the euphemism for bloody. Zola spoke out at the end of an illustrious career at a time when social re-volution was imminent. Sartre was sufficient artist to have his plays divorced from open propaganda. In Germany, after the Second World War, writers influenced by Bertolt Brecht resorted to documentary dramas which were presentations of court room evidence and historical fact. Rolf Hochhuth's *The Deputy* accused the Pope for failure to speak out against Hitler's extermination of the Jews. *The Soldiers* was an indictment of Winston Churchill for complicity in the death of General Sikorsky. Peter Weiss's *The Investigation* is a retelling of the Auschwitz trials reminding the German people and the rest of the world that silence is also an act of commitment. In each case the theatre was transformed into a political weapon, the conscience of the people, the place for public atonement of guilt. The events treated had occurred in the past and the heated partisanship lacked the scope of the more subtle influence of a work of art.

The German plays are now safely ensconced in the archives. *Waiting for Godot* will outlive *The Deputy*. It is doubtful in any case to what extent a play can influence events. The role of the artist in reaching men's minds may be more enduring than that of the editorial chronicle. Beckett, eschewing politics, probed more deeply into the breakdown of a civilization and generated an awareness of the fundamental sterility of contemporary life which unites all members of Western society. His is a call to recognition of a situation beyond politics. Ionesco is possible only in an age when technology and reason have rendered accumulated tradition no longer serviceable, when the natural sciences have failed to offer an understanding of man in his totality, when alone in the indifferent immensity of the universe, man as a self-transcendent creature has to choose between the abyss and the new enlightenment. Ionesco has steadfastly maintained that immediate political issues are transient and trivial and in the final analysis a surrender to the reign of Reason. His contribution rests on a different level.

Political action assumes a continuing social order. Aristotle could discuss the transgression of Oedipus or Antigone in the light of a social harmony blessed by the gods which had to be preserved. The correct path, plausible in an age of commonly held belief, can become self-righteous as with Arthur Miller in his earlier plays. Richelieu in a seventeenth-century governmental interference with art laid down the Rules for dramatists to follow which so circumscribed a writer's freedom that only Racine could function comfortably. Behind the Rules lay the unquestioned acceptance of absolute monarchy. In the Soviet Union socialist realism is the official art form, the most thorough example of a government decree defining the role of the artist in society. No plays of international significance have resulted. In Communist Poland, *Waiting for Godot* has political repercussions and is regarded as realistic drama. When presented in San Quentin Prison, Beckett's play had little difficulty in establishing a comprehensible relationship with its audience.

Today's revolution in manners and morals does not rely on absolutes or certainty. All is subject to doubt. Living with endless relativity may be disturbing and a writer may retreat to a defense of what was, as is the case of T. S. Eliot, Graham Greene or

Montherlant. Or he may advocate a social reorganization which presumably will establish a new order, as is the case with Bertolt Brecht and Marxism or Jean Genet and criminality. Or he may refrain from omniscience and present the chaos of continuing doubt. Ionesco offers the refreshing confirmation of the limits of Reason and the advice to choose the reality of the imagination. To do so the characters and structure of realistic drama are inadequate.

The most significant plays of the past two decades include *Mother Courage, The Visit, The Devil and the Good Lord, Waiting for Godot, The Balcony, The Death of a Salesman* and *The Killer,* widely differing in political implications. *The Balcony* offers the perverse admiration of the hierarchy of the brothel as salvation, *Mother Courage* presents the need to change society if human nature is to be less conditioned by the market place, *The Killer* is a fantasy of the inadequacy of Reason to save man from the nameless death which surrounds him. None of these plays involves an outright call for political action on a specific issue. None is a position paper on the war in Viet Nam, the dropping of the hydrogen bomb or the continued oppression of racial minorities.

Ionesco, most likely influenced by the London Controversy wrote *Rhinoceros,* his most outspoken anti-fascist statement. But the play is not a direct attack on Hitlerism but on all totalitarian society. It is a poetic metaphor exposing the dangers of mass acceptance of regimentation. It is Ionesco's final contribution to the debate on political involvement and as a work of art is far more effective than persistent pamphleteering potshots. As with *Waiting for Godot,* its political impact as a cry against conformity and submission to logic depends on time, place and audience. In his later plays, *Exit the King, Massacre Games,* and *Hunger and Thirst,* Ionesco returned to the disturbing anguish of loneliness and death.

1

(The following is excerpted from Kenneth Tynan's article on "Ionesco: Man of Destiny," which appeared in *The Observer*, June 27, 1958.)

But it was only when M. Ionesco arrived that they hailed a messiah. Here at last was a self-proclaimed advocate of *anti-théâtre:* explicitly anti-realist, and by implication anti-reality as well. Here was a writer ready to declare that words were meaningless and that all communication between human beings was impossible. The aged (as in *The Chairs*) are wrapped in an impenetrable cocoon of hallucinatory memories; they can speak intelligibly neither to each other nor to the world. The teacher in *The Lesson* can get through to his pupil only by means of sexual assault, followed by murder. Words, the magic innovation of our species, are dismissed as useless and fraudulent.

Ionesco's is a world of isolated robots, conversing in cartoon-strip balloons of dialogue that are sometimes hilarious, sometimes evocative, and quite often neither, on which occasions they become profoundly tiresome. (As with shaggy-dog stories, few of M. Ionesco's plays survive a second hearing: I felt this particularly with *The Chairs*.) This world is not mine, but I recognize it to be a valid personal vision, presented with great imaginative aplomb and verbal audacity. The peril arises when it is held up for general emulation as the gateway to the theatre of the future, that bleak new world from which all the humanist heresies of faith in logic and belief in man will forever be banished.

M. Ionesco certainly offers an "escape from realism": but an escape into what? A blind alley, perhaps, adorned with *tachiste* murals. Or a self-imposed vacuum, wherein the author ominously bids us observe the absence of air. Or, best of all, a funfair ride on a ghost train, all skulls and hooting waxworks, from which we emerge into the far more intimidating clamor of diurnal reality. M. Ionesco's theatre is pungent and exciting, but it remains a diversion. It is not on the main road: and we do him no good, nor the drama at large, to pretend that it is . . .

(The following is taken from Ionesco's reply to Kenneth Tynan in *The Observer*, July 4, 1958.)

A work of art has nothing to do with doctrine. I have already written elsewhere that any work of art which was ideological and nothing else would be pointless, tautological, inferior to the doctrine it claimed to illustrate, which would already have been expressed in its proper language, that of discursive demonstration. An ideological play can be no more than the vulgarization of an ideology. In my view, a work of art has its own unique system of expression, its own means of directly apprehending the real.

Mr. Tynan seems to accuse me of being deliberately, explicitly, anti-realist; of having declared that words have no meaning and that all language is incommunicable. That is only partly true, for the very fact of writing and presenting plays is surely incompatible with such a view. I simply hold that it is difficult to make oneself understood, not absolutely impossible, and my play *The Chairs* is a plea, pathetic perhaps, for mutual understanding. As for the idea of reality, Mr. Tynan seems (as he also made clear in an interview published in *Encounter*) to acknowledge only one plane of reality: what is called the "social" plane, which seems to me to be the most external, in other words the most superficial. That is why I think that writers like Sartre (Sartre the author of political melodramas), Osborne, Miller, Brecht, etc., are simply the new *auteurs du boulevard,* representatives of a left-wing conformism which is just as lamentable as the right-wing sort. These writers offer nothing that one does not know already, through books and political speeches. . . .

If I may be allowed to express myself paradoxically, I should say that the true society, the authentic human community, is extra-social—a wider, deeper society, that which is revealed by our common anxieties, our desires, our secret nostalgias. The whole history of the world has been governed by these nostalgias and anxieties, which political action does no more than reflect and interpret, very imperfectly. No society has been able to abolish human sadness, no political system can deliver us from

the pain of living, from our fear of death, our thrist for the
absolute; it is the human condition that directs the social condition, not vice versa. . . . The absence of ideology in a work does
not mean an absence of ideas: on the contrary it fertilizes them.
In other words, it was not Sophocles who was inspired by Freud
but, obviously, the other way round. Ideology is not the source
of art. A work of art is the source and the raw material of
ideologies to come.

What, then, should the critic do? Where should he look for
his criteria? Inside the work itself, its universe and its mythology.
He must look at it, listen to it, and simply say whether it is true
to its own nature. The best judgment is a careful exposition of
the work itself. For that, the work must be allowed to speak, un-
colored by preconception or prejudice. Whether or not it is on
the "main road" whether or not it is what you would like it to be
—to consider this is already to pass judgment, a judgment that
is external, pointless and false. A work of art is the expression of
an incommunicable reality that one tries to communicate—and
which sometimes can be communicated. That is its paradox, and
its truth.

3

(Philip Toynbee reviewing Arthur Miller's plays on July 6, 1958, joined the
attack on Ionesco.)

An Attitude To Life (Extracts)

In last week's *Observer* M. Eugène Ionesco wrote as follows:
". . . writers like Sartre, Osborne, Miller, Brecht, etc., are simply
the new *auteurs du boulevard,* representatives of a left-wing conformism which is just as lamentable as the right wing sort. These
writers offer nothing that one does not know already, through
books and political speeches." He went on to write: "I believe
that what separates us all from one another is simply society itself,
or if you like, politics. This is what raises barriers between men,
this is what creates misunderstanding."

The first of these quotations strongly suggests that Sartre is the only playwright M. Ionesco has read or seen of those whom he has chosen to attack. It certainly seems unlikely that M. Ionesco is well acquainted with the work of Arthur Miller, for the charge against him of "left-wing conformism" is as absurd as it would be to charge M. Ionesco with being the mouthpiece of the Algerian *colons.*

As for the second quotation from M. Ionesco's article, it seems to me to underline, by its frivolity, one of the very qualities which make Arthur Miller an important playwright and Eugene Ionesco a lesser one. To write that what separates us all from one another is simply "society itself" (*le social*) is like writing that the human race is horribly hampered in its freedom of movement by the atmosphere which lies so heavy on our planet.

4

(Orson Welles joined in the debate and what follows are excerpts from his article in *The Observer* July 13, 1958.)

Can the artist evade politics? He should certainly avoid polemics. Directing the course of the world, writes M. Ionesco, "is the business of the founders of religions, of the moralists or the politicians." An artist's every word is an expression of a social attitude; and I cannot agree with M. Ionesco that these expressions are always less original than political speeches or pamphlets. An artist must confirm the values of his society; or he must challenge them . . .

That politics is best left to the professionals is a perfectly respectable conservative argument; but M. Ionesco was careful to add that in his view the politicians "make a pretty poor job of it." I wish it could be said that these two sentiments—the revolutionary and the legitimist—cancel each other out. But M. Ionesco, for once, is not talking Jabberwocky: he is talking surrender.

To denounce leadership as incompetent, and, having done so, then to insist that the "direction" of world affairs be left strictly in these incompetent hands, is to acknowledge an extraordinary despair.

Under the present circumstances, the call to abandon ship is not merely unpractical: it is a cry of panic. If we are doomed indeed, let M. Ionesco go down fighting with the rest of us. He should have the courage of our platitudes.

Ionesco and La Vase

IN February 1972 *La Vase* (Slime), the first motion picture by Eugene Ionesco, was shown at the Cinémathèque Français in Paris. Ionesco not only wrote the script but is the only actor to appear in it. While resting at a Swiss spa he had secretly worked with the German director Heinz van Cramer and hoped to spring a sensational surprise in time for the film to be included in the Cannes Film Festival.

The eighty-minute film begins with a detailed examination of Ionesco trying on hats and sweaters in front of a mirror as he hums different popular tunes. The camera focuses on his facial gestures, his detailed examination of his wrinkles, the preparation of his toilette as he gets ready to take a walk in the countryside.

(The following is taken from the review by Thomas Quinn Curtiss which appeared in the New York Times, February 23, 1972.)

These promenades are filled with mishaps of a Buster Keaton nature. Mr. Ionesco's clothes are spattered by passing vehicles, he loses his umbrella in a mud puddle and his briefcase slips from under his arm, spilling his manuscripts out to be scattered by the wind. When he relaxes on a chair in a pasture, cows come to munch beside him.

At home he is equally harassed. All his optimism crumbles in the oppressive hugger-mugger of his house, where his study is littered with unanswered letters and the dining room table is strewn with unwashed dishes. His sleep is disturbed by early morning hammering and the roar of express trains. At night he is troubled by insomnia and huddles blanketed in a rocker, visited night after night by depressing visions.

In his mind's eye he sees pollution's havoc: the faucets of a sink rusted and the basin clogged with scum; flowers withered into dusty husks. At other times he imagines that he is energetically engaged in a sudden pull-yourself-together program. He rises zestfully and breakfasts with appetite, but when he tackles his neglected correspondence he hurls crumpled attempts at letter-writing one after another into the empty fire grate.

In the final reel Mr. Ionesco undertakes a mountain climb. He falls, and lies injured and forgotten on the banks of a stagnant pond.

He apparently dies and disintegrates, his remains decomposing as they float on the slimy water.

"Of course, I've missed everything and done everything wrong," remarks his off-screen voice. But he has a consoling belief in the eternal return and in the last shot the corpselike Ionesco opens an eye and blinks from under a cover of weeds.

Index

(The works of Ionesco are listed under his name)